Cross-Platform Programming with JavaScript & TypeScript

Create High-Performance Apps Using React Native, Electron, and Node.js

Thompson Carter

Rafael Sanders

Miguel Farmer

Contents

Chapter 4: Exploring Node.js for Backend Development 76

Chapter 6: Integrating React Native and Electron 122

Chapter 7: Mastering Data Synchronization . 143

[11]

[12]

Final Thoughts and Inspiration for the Future

How to Scan a Barcode to Get a Repository

1. **Install a QR/Barcode Scanner** – Ensure you have a barcode or QR code scanner app installed on your smartphone or use a built-in scanner in **GitHub, GitLab, or Bitbucket.**

2. **Open the Scanner** – Launch the scanner app and grant necessary camera permissions.

3. **Scan the Barcode** – Align the barcode within the scanning frame. The scanner will automatically detect and process it.

4. **Follow the Link** – The scanned result will display a **URL to the repository**. Tap the link to open it in your web browser or Git client.

5. **Clone the Repository** – Use **Git clone** with the provided **URL** to download the repository to your local machine.

Chapter 1: Introduction to Cross-Platform Programming

In the ever-evolving world of software development, the demand for efficient, high-performance applications is higher than ever. Developers are tasked with creating apps that not only run well on multiple platforms but also do so efficiently, ensuring users have a seamless experience, regardless of their device or operating system. This is where **cross-platform programming** comes into play. In this chapter, we'll explore what cross-platform programming really means, why JavaScript and TypeScript are excellent choices for this task, and introduce three key technologies—React Native, Electron, and Node.js—that will help streamline your development process.

What Cross-Platform Programming Really Means

At its core, **cross-platform programming** is the practice of writing code once and using it across multiple platforms, such as iOS, Android, Windows, macOS, and Linux. Traditionally, building software for different platforms required separate codebases for each one. Developers would need to write specific code tailored to each operating system's language and environment. This process was time-consuming, error-prone, and expensive.

In cross-platform development, however, you write your application once, and it runs on multiple platforms without requiring a complete rewrite for each. By using cross-platform development frameworks and tools, developers can save significant time and resources, while delivering apps that reach a wider audience.

The Benefits of Cross-Platform Development

- **Reduced Development Time:** Rather than writing separate code for each platform, cross-platform development allows you to write a single codebase. This significantly reduces the time it takes to develop and maintain your app.

- **Cost Efficiency:** Since you only need to write one set of code, you also cut down on the cost of hiring separate teams for iOS, Android, or desktop development.

- **Consistency Across Platforms:** With one codebase, ensuring that your app functions consistently across all platforms becomes easier. There are fewer discrepancies in behavior and appearance from platform to platform.

- **Wider Audience Reach:** Cross-platform apps can be deployed on multiple operating systems, reaching a broader audience without extra effort.

Consider a **restaurant reservation app** that needs to run on iOS, Android, and web browsers. Instead of hiring three different development teams, you could write the app once using a cross-platform framework, such as React Native, and deploy it across iOS, Android, and the web.

Cross-Platform Development in Practice:

- **Example 1:** A mobile app for task management could be developed with React Native, which allows it to run seamlessly on both Android and iOS with a single codebase.

- **Example 2:** A desktop application for project collaboration can be created using

Electron, providing support for Windows, macOS, and Linux.

The power of cross-platform development lies in the tools and frameworks available to developers. It's not just about saving time—it's about making the entire development process more efficient, faster, and scalable.

Choosing JavaScript and TypeScript for the Job

Now that we understand the concept and benefits of cross-platform programming, let's take a look at why **JavaScript** and **TypeScript** are the top choices for building cross-platform apps.

Why JavaScript?

JavaScript is one of the most widely used programming languages in the world. It runs natively in web browsers, making it a prime choice for building both client-side and server-side applications. JavaScript has extensive support in the cross-platform development world, especially when working with frameworks like **React Native** and **Electron**.

Here are the key reasons why JavaScript shines in cross-platform development:

1. **Ubiquity:** JavaScript is supported across all major platforms, including mobile, desktop, and web. This makes it an excellent candidate for building apps that work everywhere.

2. **Single Language for Front-End and Back-End:** JavaScript allows developers to work with both the front-end (user interface) and back-end (server-side logic) of an app. This means you don't need to learn multiple languages to build your entire application.

3. **Vibrant Ecosystem:** JavaScript has a rich ecosystem with libraries, tools, and community support that can help solve almost any development challenge.

4. **Real-Time Applications:** JavaScript, through frameworks like **Node.js**, is particularly strong at handling real-time communication, making it perfect for chat apps, live feeds, and collaborative tools.

Why TypeScript?

TypeScript is a superset of JavaScript that adds static typing to the language. It compiles down to plain JavaScript, meaning you can use it anywhere JavaScript runs. It's increasingly becoming the go-to language for cross-platform developers. Here's why:

1. **Static Typing:** TypeScript's type system can help catch errors early in the development

process, making code more predictable and less prone to bugs.

2. **Better Tooling:** TypeScript provides enhanced code completion, refactoring, and debugging tools, improving the development experience.

3. **Improved Readability and Maintainability:** Static types make the code easier to understand and maintain, especially for larger codebases or when multiple developers are involved.

4. **Compatibility with JavaScript:** Since TypeScript is a superset of JavaScript, it's easy to transition from JavaScript to TypeScript or to use both in the same project.

For example, in a project where you need to handle user authentication (a typical cross-platform use case), TypeScript helps you define types for different authentication responses and ensures that you don't mistakenly treat a response object as something it's not.

JavaScript vs TypeScript:

- **JavaScript** is more flexible, but it comes with the risk of runtime errors that are only discovered when the app is executed.

- **TypeScript**, while offering more structure and safety through its type system, may require a steeper learning curve for beginners. However, once the developer gets comfortable, TypeScript can lead to better maintainability and fewer bugs.

For many cross-platform developers, the combination of **JavaScript** and **TypeScript** provides a robust toolkit that is efficient, scalable, and maintainable across platforms.

Setting the Scene: React Native, Electron, and Node.js

Let's now introduce the three key technologies that we'll be working with in this book: **React Native**, **Electron**, and **Node.js**. These technologies will enable you to build mobile, desktop, and server-side applications that work seamlessly across platforms.

React Native: Building Cross-Platform Mobile Apps

React Native is a popular framework for building mobile applications using JavaScript and React. The beauty of React Native lies in its ability to write code once and deploy it across iOS and Android. Unlike traditional mobile app development, which requires separate codebases for different platforms, React Native allows you to use the same code for both iOS and Android, saving development time and effort.

- **How React Native Works:** React Native uses **native components** for rendering UI elements on both iOS and Android, making the app feel like a true native app, while still being able to reuse code across platforms.

- **Real-World Example:** A fitness tracking app that records exercise data and syncs with the cloud can be developed using React Native, ensuring users on both iOS and Android get a similar experience.

Electron: Cross-Platform Desktop Apps with Web Technologies

Electron is a framework that allows you to build cross-platform desktop applications using **HTML, CSS, and JavaScript**. This means that developers can leverage their existing web development skills to create desktop applications that run on **Windows, macOS**, and **Linux**.

- **How Electron Works:** Electron uses Chromium for rendering the UI and Node.js for handling the back-end logic. This makes it possible to create powerful desktop apps while maintaining a familiar web-based development experience.

- **Real-World Example:** A markdown editor or a note-taking application can be built using Electron, providing a desktop experience on multiple operating systems with minimal code changes.

Node.js: The Backend Powerhouse

Node.js is a runtime environment that allows you to run JavaScript code on the server side. It's built on **Google's V8 engine** (the same one that powers

Chrome) and is designed to be lightweight and efficient. For cross-platform development, Node.js is particularly useful for handling real-time applications and server-side logic.

- **How Node.js Works:** Node.js uses a non-blocking, event-driven architecture, which makes it highly scalable for handling a large number of simultaneous connections. It's ideal for building APIs, managing databases, and handling asynchronous operations in real-time apps.

- **Real-World Example:** A chat application with real-time messaging can benefit from Node.js, ensuring users on different devices can exchange messages without delays.

How These Technologies Work Together

Now that we've covered each of these technologies individually, let's see how they work together. In a typical cross-platform app, React Native handles the mobile user interface, Electron is used for the desktop client, and Node.js serves as the backend API that connects both.

For example, imagine you're building an app that tracks your daily tasks. React Native would be used for the mobile app that syncs your tasks, Electron would power the desktop version of the app, and Node.js would be responsible for handling the server-side logic, such as saving the tasks to a database.

Conclusion: Cross-Platform Development Made Easy

In this chapter, we've explored the fundamentals of **cross-platform programming** and discussed the power of using **JavaScript** and **TypeScript** to create apps that work across multiple platforms. We also introduced the key technologies—**React Native**, **Electron**, and **Node.js**—that will serve as the backbone of your development process.

As we move forward in the book, you'll see how these technologies come to life in practical, hands-on projects. Cross-platform development can be a game-changer, allowing you to write code once and deploy it across iOS, Android, desktop, and web platforms, all while reducing time and cost.

Stay tuned as we dive deeper into each of these technologies and explore how to use them to create high-performance applications that meet today's development needs.

Chapter 2: Preparing Your Development Toolkit

In the world of cross-platform development, the right toolkit is essential to streamline your development process, enhance productivity, and ensure that your applications run smoothly across different platforms. This chapter will guide you through preparing your development environment with the necessary tools for success.

We'll cover installing **Node.js, npm,** and your chosen **IDE,** and show you how to set up the perfect environment for building cross-platform apps. Along the way, we'll provide hands-on examples to help you get started with your first app, so you can see how everything fits together.

Essential Tools for Cross-Platform Development

Before diving into coding, it's important to have the right tools set up. Here's what we'll focus on in this section:

1. **Node.js**

2. **npm (Node Package Manager)**

3. **Choosing Your Integrated Development Environment (IDE)**

Let's start by setting up these essential tools that will make your development process seamless and efficient.

---

1. Installing Node.js

Node.js is a runtime environment that allows you to run JavaScript on the server-side. It's an essential tool for building and running cross-platform apps, particularly those using **React Native**, **Electron**, and **Node.js** itself. It's fast, efficient, and has a large ecosystem of libraries to extend your app's functionality.

Steps to Install Node.js

1. **Visit the Node.js Website** Go to the official Node.js website: https://nodejs.org.

   You'll be presented with two options: **LTS (Long Term Support)** and **Current**. For stability and compatibility, we recommend installing the LTS version.

2. **Download   the   Installer**
Click the appropriate installer for your operating system (Windows, macOS, or Linux). If you're using Windows, you'll download a .msi file, and for macOS, a .pkg file.

3. **Run   the   Installer**
Once the installer is downloaded, open it and follow the prompts. The default options are usually fine for most users, so you can go ahead and accept them.

4. **Verify   the   Installation**
After installation, open your terminal or command prompt and type the following command:

bash

```
node -v
```

This will display the version of Node.js installed. If you see the version number, you've successfully installed Node.js!

Why Node.js is Essential

Node.js is important because it provides the backend runtime environment for your cross-platform apps, especially those built using React Native (for mobile) or Electron (for desktop). It helps you run server-side JavaScript, manage backend processes, and communicate with databases, making it a key component in full-stack cross-platform development.

2. Installing npm (Node Package Manager)

npm is the package manager for Node.js. It allows you to install and manage the libraries and dependencies your project needs. In fact, npm comes bundled with Node.js, so once you've installed Node.js, npm is already installed.

How npm Works

npm makes it easy to install open-source packages. For example, if you're using React Native for mobile app development, you can use npm to install libraries and packages that provide additional functionality, such as navigation tools or state management libraries.

Using npm to Install Packages

To install a package, use the following command in your terminal or command prompt:

```bash
```

```
npm install <package-name>
```

For example, to install React Native globally, you would run:

```
bash
```

```
npm install -g react-native-cli
```

This installs the React Native command-line interface globally, making it accessible from anywhere on your computer.

Verifying npm Installation

Just like Node.js, you can verify that npm is installed correctly by typing the following command in your terminal:

```
bash
```

```
npm -v
```

If you see the version number, npm is installed and ready to go!

3. Choosing Your Integrated Development Environment (IDE)

An Integrated Development Environment (IDE) is where you will write and manage your code. The right IDE will make your development process smoother and more efficient by providing features like syntax highlighting, code completion, and debugging tools.

Popular IDEs for Cross-Platform Development

- **Visual Studio Code (VS Code)** Visual Studio Code is one of the most popular IDEs for JavaScript and TypeScript development. It's lightweight, customizable, and comes with built-in support for Git. It has an extensive library of extensions that help with React Native, Node.js, and other technologies.

- **WebStorm**

  WebStorm is a more feature-rich, paid IDE developed by JetBrains. It provides advanced code analysis and debugging capabilities, which can be helpful for large, complex projects.

- **Atom**

  Atom is an open-source text editor developed by GitHub. It's highly customizable and works well for developers who prefer a more lightweight option.

Installing VS Code

To get started, we'll use **VS Code**, as it's free, widely used, and has excellent support for

JavaScript, TypeScript, and React Native development.

1. **Go to the Visual Studio Code Website**
   Visit https://code.visualstudio.com/ and download the installer for your operating system.

2. **Install VS Code**
   Follow the installation prompts. VS Code is lightweight and installs quickly.

3. **Install Recommended Extensions**
   After installing VS Code, you'll want to install some extensions to help with cross-platform development:

   o **React Native Tools**: For debugging and running React Native apps directly from the editor.

   o **Prettier**: For code formatting.

- o **ESLint**: To catch potential errors and enforce coding standards.

- o **TypeScript**: If you're using TypeScript, this extension provides all the language features you need.

Once you have your IDE set up, you're ready to start building cross-platform apps.

Creating Your First Cross-Platform App

Now that your development environment is set up, it's time to create your first cross-platform app. We'll start with a simple **React Native app**, which can run on both iOS and Android.

Setting Up Your First React Native Project

1. **Install React Native CLI**

   If you haven't already installed the React Native command-line interface (CLI), you can do so using npm:

```bash
```

```bash
npm install -g react-native-cli
```

2. **Create a New React Native Project**

   Once the CLI is installed, create a new React Native project by running the following command:

```bash
```

```bash
npx react-native init MyFirstApp
```

This will create a new folder called MyFirstApp with all the necessary files and dependencies for a React Native project.

3. **Navigate to Your Project Directory**
Change your terminal's directory to the
newly created project folder:

```bash

cd MyFirstApp
```

4. **Run the App on an Emulator or Physical Device**
To see your app in action, you can run it
either on an Android or iOS emulator, or
on a physical device.

For Android, run:

```bash

npx react-native run-android
```

For iOS (on macOS only), run:

```bash

npx react-native run-ios
```

This will launch the app in your emulator or on your connected device.

Understanding the Code Structure

Once the app is running, let's take a look at the basic file structure of a React Native project:

- **/android/** – Contains the native Android project files.

- **/ios/** – Contains the native iOS project files.

- **/node_modules/** – Stores all the npm packages your project depends on.

- **App.js** – The main entry point for your app. This is where the code for the app's user interface (UI) lives.

Here's an example of a basic **App.js** file that displays "Hello, World!" on the screen:

```
javascript
```

```
import React from 'react';
import { SafeAreaView, Text } from
'react-native';

const App = () => {
  return (
    <SafeAreaView>
      <Text>Hello, World!</Text>
    </SafeAreaView>
  );
};

export default App;
```

This is just a starting point. As you continue to explore React Native, you'll learn how to add more features and create more complex UIs.

Navigating the Development Process

Now that your first app is up and running, it's important to understand how to navigate the development process effectively. Organizing your workspace and project files efficiently is key to creating maintainable, scalable applications.

Understanding Your Project Files

As you dive deeper into building cross-platform apps, you'll encounter various files and directories. Here's a breakdown of the key ones:

- **package.json** – This file contains metadata about your project, such as dependencies, scripts, and project settings.

- **/src/** – This is where you'll store most of your app's code (components, functions, etc.).

- **App.js** – The main entry point for the app, where your app's UI components and logic are defined.

Organizing Your Codebase

As your app grows, you'll need to organize your code to maintain clarity and scalability. A common approach is to divide the app into **components** and **screens**:

- **components/** – Reusable UI elements (e.g., buttons, headers).

- **screens/** – Larger views that represent individual screens in the app (e.g., home screen, settings screen).

Here's an example of how you might organize your app:

```bash

/src
```

```
/components
    Button.js
    Header.js
/screens
    HomeScreen.js
    SettingsScreen.js
App.js
```

This structure helps keep the code clean and organized, making it easier to scale as your app grows.

Conclusion

Congratulations! You've successfully set up your development environment and created your first React Native app. By installing Node.js, npm, and choosing the right IDE (VS Code), you've equipped yourself with the essential tools needed to build powerful cross-platform applications. You've also learned how to navigate the development process and organize your codebase effectively.

In the next chapter, we'll dive deeper into React Native and explore how to create dynamic, interactive apps with advanced features. Keep experimenting with your current app, and don't hesitate to build on what you've learned so far. Cross-platform development is an exciting journey, and you're well on your way to becoming a skilled developer!

Chapter 3: Deep Dive into React Native

In this chapter, we are going to take a deep dive into **React Native**, one of the most popular frameworks for building mobile applications that work seamlessly across both iOS and Android. We'll explore its core principles, walk through building a simple app, and then show you how to debug and test your app effectively. Whether you're new to mobile development or just new to React Native, this chapter is designed to help you understand the foundational concepts and build a functional mobile app that you can proudly showcase.

React Native Unveiled: Mobile Development Made Simple

React Native is a powerful framework that allows developers to use **JavaScript** and **React** to build mobile apps for both iOS and Android. What makes React Native different is its ability to use a single codebase for both platforms, dramatically reducing development time and effort.

React Native works by using **native components** to render the user interface (UI). This means that, unlike hybrid mobile app frameworks (which rely on WebViews to display content), React Native compiles to actual native code, resulting in apps that feel and perform like native apps.

Core Principles of React Native

1. Components and JSX: Building the UI

In React Native, the UI is built using **components,** which are the building blocks of your application. Components can be either

functional or **class-based,** but with modern React (and React Native), **functional components** are preferred due to their simplicity and ease of use with **React Hooks.**

JSX (JavaScript XML) is the syntax used to define components. It allows you to write HTML-like code within JavaScript. React Native components are written using JSX, and they map directly to native UI elements.

Example of JSX in React Native:

```javascript
import React from 'react';
import { Text, View } from 'react-native';

const App = () => {
  return (
```

```
    <View style={{ flex: 1,
justifyContent: 'center',
alignItems: 'center' }}>
    <Text>Hello, World!</Text>
    </View>
  );
};


export default App;
```

In this example:

- o The \<View\> component is similar to a div in HTML. It is a container for other elements.

- o The \<Text\> component is used to display text in your app.

This simple app will render a text message in the center of the screen.

2. **Managing State in React Native**

Managing the state of your app is crucial to creating dynamic, interactive user experiences. **State** refers to the data that determines the rendering of your components. In React Native, you can manage state using React's built-in **useState hook** or **class component state**.

For functional components, **useState** is the go-to solution for handling state.

Example of State Management with useState:

javascript

```
import React, { useState } from
'react';
import { View, Text, Button } from
'react-native';

const App = () => {
  const [count, setCount] =
useState(0);
```

```
  return (
    <View style={{ flex: 1,
justifyContent: 'center',
alignItems: 'center' }}>
      <Text>You clicked {count}
times</Text>
      <Button title="Click me"
onPress={() => setCount(count +
1)} />
    </View>
  );
};


export default App;
```

In this example:

- o count is the state variable.

- o setCount is the function that updates count.

- o When the user presses the "Click me" button, the count is incremented.

3. Styling in React Native

React Native uses **StyleSheet** to apply styles to components. It's similar to how you'd use CSS in web development, but instead of traditional CSS syntax, React Native uses JavaScript to define styles.

Example of Styling with StyleSheet:

```javascript
import React from 'react';
import { Text, View, StyleSheet }
from 'react-native';

const App = () => {
  return (
```

```
    <View
style={styles.container}>
      <Text
style={styles.text}>Hello,
World!</Text>
    </View>
  );
};


const styles = StyleSheet.create({
  container: {
    flex: 1,
    justifyContent: 'center',
    alignItems: 'center',
    backgroundColor: 'lightblue',
  },
  text: {
    fontSize: 24,
    color: 'darkblue',
  },
});
```

```
export default App;
```

Here, the styles are separated into a StyleSheet object, making the code cleaner and more maintainable. You can also use inline styles, but using StyleSheet is preferred for performance reasons.

Project: Building Your First React Native App

In this section, we'll walk through a **hands-on project** where you'll build a **simple to-do list app** with React Native. This app will help you understand how to handle user inputs, update the UI, and interact with local storage for persisting data.

Step 1: Set Up the Project

1. **Create a New React Native Project:**

Open your terminal and run the following command to create a new React Native project:

bash

```
npx react-native init TodoApp
```

Navigate into the project folder:

bash

```
cd TodoApp
```

2. **Run the App:**

To ensure everything is set up correctly, run the app in your emulator or on a physical device:

For Android:

bash

```
npx react-native run-android
```

For iOS (on macOS):

```bash
bash
```

```bash
npx react-native run-ios
```

Step 2: Building the To-Do List UI

Start by building the user interface. The app will have:

- A text input field for adding tasks.

- A button to add tasks.

- A list to display tasks.

Here's the code to create this UI:

```javascript
javascript

import React, { useState } from
'react';
import { View, Text, TextInput,
Button, FlatList, StyleSheet }
from 'react-native';
```

```
const App = () => {
  const [task, setTask] =
useState('');
  const [tasks, setTasks] =
useState([]);

  const addTask = () => {
    if (task) {
      setTasks([...tasks, { key:
Math.random().toString(), value:
task }]);
      setTask('');
    }
  };

  return (
    <View
style={styles.container}>
```

```
    <Text
style={styles.header}>To-Do
List</Text>
    <TextInput
      style={styles.input}
      placeholder="Enter a task"
      value={task}
      onChangeText={setTask}
    />
    <Button title="Add Task"
onPress={addTask} />
    <FlatList
      data={tasks}
      renderItem={(itemData) =>
(
        <View
style={styles.listItem}>

<Text>{itemData.item.value}</Text>
        </View>
      )}
```

```
        />
      </View>
    );
};


const styles = StyleSheet.create({
    container: {
      flex: 1,
      padding: 50,
      justifyContent: 'center',
      backgroundColor: '#fff',
    },
    header: {
      fontSize: 28,
      marginBottom: 10,
    },
    input: {
      width: '80%',
      borderColor: '#ccc',
      borderWidth: 1,
      padding: 10,
```

```
    marginBottom: 10,
  },
  listItem: {
    padding: 10,
    borderBottomColor: '#ccc',
    borderBottomWidth: 1,
  },
});


export default App;
```

In this code:

- The TextInput component allows the user to type tasks.

- The Button component triggers the function to add tasks to the list.

- FlatList is used to display the list of tasks dynamically.

Step 3: Handling Local Storage

To persist the tasks even when the app is closed, we can use React Native's **AsyncStorage** to store the data locally.

1. **Install AsyncStorage:**

Run the following command to install @react-native-async-storage/async-storage:

```bash
bash
```

```bash
npm install @react-native-async-storage/async-storage
```

2. **Implement AsyncStorage to Persist Data:**

Update your App.js file to include AsyncStorage. We'll modify the app to save and retrieve tasks from local storage.

```javascript
javascript
```

```
import React, { useState,
useEffect } from 'react';
import { View, Text, TextInput,
Button, FlatList, StyleSheet }
from 'react-native';
import AsyncStorage from '@react-
native-async-storage/async-
storage';

const App = () => {
  const [task, setTask] =
useState('');
  const [tasks, setTasks] =
useState([]);

  useEffect(() => {
    // Load tasks from
AsyncStorage on app load
    const loadTasks = async () =>
{
      try {
```

```
      const storedTasks = await
AsyncStorage.getItem('tasks');
      if (storedTasks) {

setTasks(JSON.parse(storedTasks));
      }
    } catch (error) {
      console.error('Failed to
load tasks from storage', error);
      }
    };

  loadTasks();
  }, []);

  const addTask = async () => {
    if (task) {
      const newTasks = [...tasks,
{ key: Math.random().toString(),
value: task }];
      setTasks(newTasks);
```

```
setTask('');
try {
  // Store tasks in
AsyncStorage
  await
AsyncStorage.setItem('tasks',
JSON.stringify(newTasks));
} catch (error) {
  console.error('Failed to
save task', error);
}
}
};


return (
  <View
style={styles.container}>
    <Text
style={styles.header}>To-Do
List</Text>
    <TextInput
```

```
      style={styles.input}
      placeholder="Enter a task"
      value={task}
      onChangeText={setTask}
    />
    <Button title="Add Task"
onPress={addTask} />
    <FlatList
      data={tasks}
      renderItem={(itemData) =>
(
        <View
style={styles.listItem}>

<Text>{itemData.item.value}</Text>
        </View>
      )}
    />
  </View>
 );
};
```

```
const styles = StyleSheet.create({
  container: {
    flex: 1,
    padding: 50,
    justifyContent: 'center',
    backgroundColor: '#fff',
  },
  header: {
    fontSize: 28,
    marginBottom: 10,
  },
  input: {
    width: '80%',
    borderColor: '#ccc',
    borderWidth: 1,
    padding: 10,
    marginBottom: 10,
  },
  listItem: {
    padding: 10,
```

```
    borderBottomColor: '#ccc',
    borderBottomWidth: 1,
  },
});
```

```
export default App;
```

With these changes, the to-do list will persist even after the app is closed and reopened.

Debugging and Testing React Native Apps

Debugging is a critical part of the development process, especially when building mobile apps. React Native provides several tools to help you identify and fix issues in your code.

Using React Native Debugger

1. **Remote Debugging:** React Native has built-in remote debugging tools. To enable

them, press **Cmd + D (iOS)** or **Cmd + M (Android)** to open the developer menu and select **Debug**. This will open a Chrome window with debugging tools.

2. **React Native Debugger:** A standalone app that combines Redux DevTools and Chrome DevTools for debugging React Native apps.

Install it via:

bash

```
brew install react-native-debugger
```
Open it, then start your app and connect to the debugger.

Conclusion

In this chapter, we've taken a deep dive into React Native, covering the key concepts that will allow you to build and manage mobile applications. You've learned how to:

- Build a simple to-do list app with React Native.

- Manage state, handle user inputs, and display dynamic content.

- Persist data using AsyncStorage.

- Debug your app using powerful tools like React Native Debugger.

Now that you have the foundation, you can start building more complex and interactive apps. Keep experimenting, testing, and refining your skills as you move on to more advanced topics in

mobile development. You're on your way to becoming a proficient React Native developer!

Chapter 4: Exploring Node.js for Backend Development

In today's world of web and mobile applications, backend development is just as important as the front-end. The backend is responsible for managing data, handling user requests, performing server-side logic, and providing essential functionality to the application. **Node.js** is one of the most popular technologies for backend development, and in this chapter, we will explore its core features, why it is so effective, and how to use it to build scalable and efficient backend applications. Additionally, we will walk through a hands-on project where you'll create a **RESTful API** using **Node.js**, **Express**, and

MongoDB, and finally, connect that backend to your **React Native** app to sync data.

What is Node.js and Why Should You Use It?

Node.js is an open-source, event-driven runtime environment that enables developers to run JavaScript on the server side. It uses **Google's V8 JavaScript engine**, the same engine used by Google Chrome, to execute code quickly and efficiently. Node.js allows you to build scalable, high-performance applications that are capable of handling multiple simultaneous connections. Unlike traditional server-side technologies, Node.js operates on a **non-blocking, event-driven architecture**, which makes it ideal for I/O-heavy applications like web servers and real-time applications.

Core Features of Node.js

Let's take a closer look at the key features of Node.js:

1. Non-Blocking, Event-Driven Architecture

The heart of Node.js lies in its **non-blocking, event-driven model.** This means that instead of waiting for one operation to complete before moving on to the next (like in traditional server-side applications), Node.js uses events to handle multiple operations concurrently.

Analogy: Imagine you are at a fast-food restaurant. A traditional approach would be like having the cook prepare one order at a time (blocking). In contrast, Node.js is like a restaurant where multiple orders are being prepared at once, and the server only checks back once the food is ready (non-blocking). This allows Node.js to handle multiple requests without slowing down the process.

2. Single-Threaded Model

Node.js operates on a **single-threaded event loop**, which handles requests one at a time. While this might sound limiting, it actually helps Node.js scale more efficiently than traditional multithreaded systems. Instead of creating a new thread for each incoming request (which can quickly consume a lot of resources), Node.js uses asynchronous callbacks to process requests in the background, freeing up the thread to handle other operations.

3. Fast Performance with V8 Engine

Node.js uses the **V8 JavaScript engine**, which is optimized for fast execution. The V8 engine compiles JavaScript directly into machine code, rather than interpreting it line by line, making it very fast compared to traditional server-side languages.

4. Built-in Modules

Node.js comes with a variety of **built-in modules** for common backend tasks. These modules simplify the development process by eliminating the need for external libraries. For example, you can use the **http** module to create a simple web server, or the **fs** module to interact with the file system.

5. Package Management with npm

npm (Node Package Manager) is the default package manager for Node.js. It allows you to easily install, update, and manage third-party libraries and dependencies for your Node.js project. With access to millions of libraries in the npm registry, you can quickly add powerful features to your application without reinventing the wheel.

Why Node.js is Ideal for Scalable Server-Side Applications

Node.js is particularly well-suited for applications that require high concurrency and real-time interaction. Here are some key use cases:

- **Real-Time Applications:** Applications like chat apps, live feeds, and gaming applications rely on constant data flow between the client and server. Node.js is ideal for these use cases because of its event-driven, non-blocking architecture, which allows it to handle large volumes of simultaneous connections with low latency.

- **APIs for Mobile and Web Apps:** Node.js is great for building APIs that interact with mobile and web applications. It can efficiently handle a large number of API requests and integrate seamlessly with databases, making it a popular choice for RESTful and GraphQL APIs.

- **Microservices Architecture:** Node.js's lightweight nature makes it an excellent choice for building microservices. You can build small, modular services that communicate with each other over HTTP, WebSockets, or messaging queues.

In summary, Node.js is ideal for building fast, scalable, and efficient backend applications that need to handle multiple simultaneous connections, real-time interactions, and large volumes of data.

Hands-on Project: Building a RESTful API

Now that we understand the basics of Node.js, let's dive into a practical example by building a **RESTful API**. This API will allow a mobile app to interact with a backend server and perform CRUD (Create, Read, Update, Delete) operations on a list of tasks.

Step 1: Setting Up Your Project

To start, we'll create a simple **Node.js** project with **Express** (a popular web framework for Node.js) and **MongoDB** (a NoSQL database).

1. Create a New Node.js Project

Open your terminal and run the following commands to create a new project folder and initialize it:

bash

```
mkdir todo-api
cd todo-api
npm init -y
```

This will generate a package.json file, which will store information about your project and its dependencies.

2. Install Dependencies

Next, install the necessary dependencies: **Express** (for routing and middleware), **Mongoose** (for interacting with MongoDB), and **Cors** (to handle cross-origin requests):

bash

```
npm install express mongoose cors
```

Step 2: Create a Basic Express Server

Let's start by creating a basic server that listens for incoming requests.

Create a file called server.js in the root of your project folder and add the following code:

```
javascript
```

```javascript
const express =
require('express');
const cors = require('cors');
const mongoose =
require('mongoose');

// Initialize Express app
const app = express();
```

```
// Middleware
app.use(cors());
app.use(express.json());  // Parse
incoming JSON requests


// Connect to MongoDB
mongoose.connect('mongodb://localh
ost:27017/todoApp', {
  useNewUrlParser: true,
  useUnifiedTopology: true,
})
.then(() => console.log('Connected
to MongoDB'))
.catch((err) =>
console.log('Failed to connect to
MongoDB', err));


// Simple route
app.get('/', (req, res) => {
  res.send('Hello from the Todo
API!');
```

```
});

// Start server
const PORT = process.env.PORT ||
5000;
app.listen(PORT, () => {
  console.log(`Server is running
on port ${PORT}`);
});
```

Here's what the code does:

- It imports **Express, Mongoose,** and **Cors.**

- It sets up an Express server that listens on port 5000.

- It connects to a **MongoDB** database called todoApp.

- It sets up a basic **GET** route that responds with a simple message.

Step 3: Defining the Task Model

Next, we'll define a **Task** model using **Mongoose**. This model will represent a task in the MongoDB database.

Create a new folder called models and add a file called Task.js:

```javascript

const mongoose =
require('mongoose');

// Define the Task schema
const taskSchema = new
mongoose.Schema({
  title: { type: String, required:
true },
  completed: { type: Boolean,
default: false },
});
```

```
// Create and export the Task
model
module.exports =
mongoose.model('Task',
taskSchema);
```

This model defines a task with two fields: **title** (a required string) and **completed** (a boolean, defaulting to false).

Step 4: Implementing CRUD Routes

Now that we have our model set up, let's implement the CRUD operations in the API.

In the server.js file, add the following routes:

```
javascript


const Task =
require('./models/Task');


// Create a new task
```

```javascript
app.post('/tasks', async (req,
res) => {
  const { title } = req.body;
  try {
    const task = new Task({ title
});
    await task.save();
    res.status(201).json(task);
  } catch (err) {
    res.status(400).json({ error:
'Failed to create task' });
  }
});

// Get all tasks
app.get('/tasks', async (req, res)
=> {
  try {
    const tasks = await
Task.find();
    res.status(200).json(tasks);
```

```javascript
  } catch (err) {
    res.status(400).json({ error:
'Failed to fetch tasks' });
  }
});

// Update a task
app.put('/tasks/:id', async (req,
res) => {
  const { id } = req.params;
  const { title, completed } =
req.body;
  try {
    const task = await
Task.findByIdAndUpdate(id, {
title, completed }, { new: true
});
    res.status(200).json(task);
  } catch (err) {
    res.status(400).json({ error:
'Failed to update task' });
```

```
    }
});


// Delete a task
app.delete('/tasks/:id', async
(req, res) => {
  const { id } = req.params;
  try {
    await
Task.findByIdAndDelete(id);
    res.status(200).json({
message: 'Task deleted' });
  } catch (err) {
    res.status(400).json({ error:
'Failed to delete task' });
  }
});
```

These routes allow you to:

- **Create** a new task (POST /tasks).

- **Read** all tasks (GET /tasks).

- **Update** an existing task (PUT /tasks/:id).

- **Delete** a task (DELETE /tasks/:id).

Step 5: Testing the API

Now that your API is set up, you can test it using **Postman** or **cURL**.

1. **Start the server** by running the following command:

```bash
```

```
node server.js
```

2. **Test the API** using Postman or cURL. For example, to create a new task, send a **POST** request to http://localhost:5000/tasks with a **JSON** body:

```json
```

```
{
```

```
"title": "Buy groceries"
}
```

Connecting the Backend with Your React Native App

With the backend API in place, it's time to connect your **React Native** app to the Node.js server to send and retrieve data.

1. Install Axios for HTTP Requests

In your React Native project, install **Axios** to make HTTP requests to your Node.js API:

```bash
bash
```

```bash
npm install axios
```

2. Fetching Data from the Backend

In your App.js file, use Axios to fetch tasks from the backend and display them in a FlatList component.

```javascript
import React, { useState,
useEffect } from 'react';
import { View, Text, FlatList,
Button, TextInput } from 'react-
native';
import axios from 'axios';

const App = () => {
  const [tasks, setTasks] =
useState([]);
  const [newTask, setNewTask] =
useState('');

  // Fetch tasks from the backend
  const fetchTasks = async () => {
    try {
      const response = await
axios.get('http://localhost:5000/t
asks');
```

```
    setTasks(response.data);
  } catch (error) {
    console.error('Error
fetching tasks', error);
  }
};


useEffect(() => {
  fetchTasks();
}, []);


// Add new task
const addTask = async () => {
  try {
    await
axios.post('http://localhost:5000/
tasks', { title: newTask });
    setNewTask('');
    fetchTasks();
  } catch (error) {
```

```
      console.error('Error adding
task', error);
    }
  };


  return (
    <View>
      <Text>Task List</Text>
      <TextInput
        placeholder="New Task"
        value={newTask}
        onChangeText={setNewTask}
      />
      <Button title="Add Task"
onPress={addTask} />
      <FlatList
        data={tasks}
        renderItem={({ item }) =>
<Text>{item.title}</Text>}
        keyExtractor={(item) =>
item._id}
```

```
    />
  </View>
  );
};
```

```
export default App;
```

In this example:

- The app fetches tasks from the backend using Axios when it loads (useEffect).

- It displays tasks in a FlatList and allows the user to add new tasks via the TextInput and Button.

Conclusion

In this chapter, you learned about **Node.js** and its key features, including its non-blocking, event-driven architecture and its ability to handle scalable applications. We also built a **RESTful**

API using **Express** and **MongoDB**, and connected that backend to a **React Native** mobile app to allow for real-time data synchronization. Now, you can expand this backend by adding user authentication, more complex data structures, and other features to make your applications more powerful and interactive.

By understanding how Node.js works and learning how to connect it with mobile applications, you've taken an important step toward becoming proficient in backend development for cross-platform apps.

Chapter 5: Crafting Desktop Apps with Electron

With the increasing demand for cross-platform applications, building desktop apps that run seamlessly across different operating systems has become essential. But what if you could use your existing web development skills to build powerful, native desktop applications? Enter **Electron**, a framework that allows you to use **web technologies** like **HTML, CSS**, and **JavaScript** to build native desktop apps for **Windows, macOS**, and **Linux**. This chapter will explain how Electron works, guide you through creating your first desktop app, and show you how to package and distribute your Electron app for different operating systems.

Electron Explained: Building Cross-Platform Desktop Apps

Electron is a powerful framework that allows developers to create desktop applications using web technologies. It combines the **Chromium engine** (for rendering web pages) and **Node.js** (for backend functionality) into a single package. This combination enables you to build cross-platform apps that have the performance of native applications but the ease of development that comes with web technologies.

What is Electron?

Electron is an open-source framework developed by **GitHub**. It essentially wraps your web application in a native shell, enabling you to run the application as a desktop app. This allows you to use familiar web technologies such as HTML, CSS, and JavaScript to develop applications that work across platforms without needing to rewrite code for each operating system.

The key components that make up Electron are:

- **Chromium:** The open-source web browser engine that Electron uses to render web pages. It's the same engine used in **Google Chrome**.

- **Node.js:** The JavaScript runtime that allows you to interact with the file system, network, and other system-level functionalities.

- **Electron APIs:** These provide access to native features like dialogs, notifications, and menus.

Electron's Architecture

Electron's architecture can be broken down into two main processes:

1. **Main Process**: This is the process that runs the core application. It manages the application lifecycle, creates windows, and integrates with native system features like file systems and hardware. The **main process** is where **Node.js** is executed.

2. **Renderer Process:** This process is responsible for displaying the user interface (UI) of the app. It runs web technologies (HTML, CSS, JavaScript) and communicates with the main process to access system resources.

The **main process** and **renderer process** communicate via **IPC (Inter-Process Communication)**. This allows the renderer to request actions like opening files or interacting with the system's clipboard, while the main process performs these actions.

Why Use Electron?

Here are some reasons why you might choose **Electron** for building desktop apps:

1. **Cross-Platform Development:** With Electron, you write your app once and deploy it on **macOS**, **Windows**, and **Linux**. This eliminates the need to learn different programming languages and frameworks for each platform.

2. **Familiar Web Technologies**: If you're already familiar with **JavaScript**, **HTML**, and **CSS**, you can leverage your existing knowledge to build desktop applications.

3. **Native Desktop Features**: Electron provides access to native operating system features, such as menus, notifications, and native file system access, making your desktop apps feel truly native.

4. **Active Community and Ecosystem**: Being open-source and widely used, Electron has a large community and a wealth of plugins, resources, and documentation to help you get started and solve problems efficiently.

Project: Building a Basic Desktop App with Electron

Now that we have an understanding of how Electron works, let's get hands-on by building a basic **note-taking app**. This project will introduce you to the core concepts of Electron, such as creating windows, handling user input, and saving data.

Step 1: Setting Up the Project

Let's start by setting up the Electron environment and creating our first project.

1. **Install Node.js**: If you haven't installed Node.js yet, download it from <u>nodejs.org</u>. This will also install **npm** (Node Package Manager), which will be used to install Electron and other dependencies.

2. **Create a New Directory for the Project:**

Open your terminal or command prompt, and create a new directory for your project:

bash

```
mkdir electron-note-app
cd electron-note-app
```

3. **Initialize the Project with npm:**

Initialize a new Node.js project with the following command:

bash

```
npm init -y
```

This will create a package.json file that contains metadata about your project and its dependencies.

4. Install Electron:

Now, install Electron as a development dependency:

bash

```
npm install electron --save-dev
```

Step 2: Create the Basic App Structure

Next, let's create the files and folders needed for the app. In your project directory, create the following structure:

bash

```
/electron-note-app
  /src
```

```
index.html
style.css
main.js
package.json
```

- **index.html**: This will be the UI of your note-taking app.

- **style.css**: The styles for the UI.

- **main.js**: The entry point for Electron, where the main process code will go.

Step 3: Set Up the Main Process

Open the main.js file and add the following code to set up the Electron main process. This code creates a window for the app and loads the index.html file into it:

```javascript
const { app, BrowserWindow } =
require('electron');
const path = require('path');
```

```
let mainWindow;

function createWindow() {
  mainWindow = new BrowserWindow({
    width: 800,
    height: 600,
    webPreferences: {
      nodeIntegration: true,
    },
  });



mainWindow.loadFile(path.join(__di
rname, 'index.html'));

  mainWindow.on('closed', () => {
    mainWindow = null;
  });
}
```

```
app.on('ready', createWindow);


app.on('window-all-closed', () =>
{
  if (process.platform !==
'darwin') {
    app.quit();
  }
});
```

Step 4: Create the User Interface (UI)

Now, open the index.html file and create a simple note-taking UI with a text area for input and a button to save notes:

```html
<!DOCTYPE html>
<html lang="en">
<head>
  <meta charset="UTF-8">
```

```
<meta name="viewport"
content="width=device-width,
initial-scale=1.0">
<title>Electron Note App</title>
<link rel="stylesheet"
href="style.css">
</head>
<body>
<div class="container">
<h1>Note-Taking App</h1>
<textarea id="note-input"
placeholder="Write your note
here..."></textarea>
<button id="save-button">Save
Note</button>
<div id="saved-notes"></div>
</div>

<script
src="renderer.js"></script>
</body>
```

```
</html>
```

Step 5: Add Styles

Open the style.css file and add some basic styles
to make the UI look nice:

css

```css
body {
  font-family: Arial, sans-serif;
  display: flex;
  justify-content: center;
  align-items: center;
  height: 100vh;
  background-color: #f4f4f9;
  margin: 0;
}

.container {
  text-align: center;
  max-width: 500px;
  width: 100%;
```

```css
}

textarea {
  width: 80%;
  height: 200px;
  margin-top: 20px;
  padding: 10px;
  font-size: 16px;
}

button {
  padding: 10px 20px;
  margin-top: 20px;
  font-size: 16px;
  cursor: pointer;
}

button:hover {
  background-color: #4CAF50;
  color: white;
}
```

```
#saved-notes {
  margin-top: 30px;
}
```

Step 6: Add Interactivity with Renderer Process

The renderer.js file will handle the interaction between the user and the app. It will save the notes and display them below the input field. Create a new file called renderer.js and add the following code:

```
javascript
```

```
const fs = require('fs');
const path = require('path');

const saveButton =
document.getElementById('save-
button');
```

```
const noteInput =
document.getElementById('note-
input');
const savedNotes =
document.getElementById('saved-
notes');

// Load saved notes from a file
function loadNotes() {
  const notesFilePath =
path.join(__dirname, 'notes.txt');
  if
(fs.existsSync(notesFilePath)) {
    const notes =
fs.readFileSync(notesFilePath,
'utf-8').split('\n');
    savedNotes.innerHTML =
notes.map(note =>
`<p>${note}</p>`).join('');
  }
}
```

```javascript
// Save the note to a file
saveButton.addEventListener('click', () => {
  const note = noteInput.value;
  if (note) {
    const notesFilePath =
path.join(__dirname, 'notes.txt');

fs.appendFileSync(notesFilePath,
note + '\n');
    loadNotes();
    noteInput.value = '';
  }
});


// Load notes when the app starts
loadNotes();
```

This script:

- Reads saved notes from a text file (notes.txt).

- Saves new notes to the same text file when the user clicks the "Save Note" button.

- Displays all saved notes in the #saved-notes section.

Packaging and Distributing Your Electron App

Once you've built your app, it's time to package it for distribution. Electron provides tools to package your app for different operating systems, and we'll use **Electron Builder** to make this process easier.

Step 1: Install Electron Builder

To package your Electron app, you need to install **Electron Builder**:

```bash
npm install electron-builder --
save-dev
```

Step 2: Update package.json

In your package.json file, add the following configurations for Electron Builder:

```json
"build": {
  "appId": "com.example.noteapp",
  "productName": "NoteApp",
  "files": [
    "**/*"
  ],
  "mac": {
    "target": "dmg"
  },
  "win": {
    "target": "nsis"
```

```
},
"linux": {
  "target": "AppImage"
}
}
```

Step 3: Package Your App

To package your app for your platform, run:

```bash
bash
```

```
npm run dist
```

This will generate executables for **macOS**, **Windows**, and **Linux**, ready for distribution.

Conclusion

In this chapter, you've learned how to build a cross-platform desktop app using **Electron**. You've explored the basics of Electron's architecture, created a simple note-taking app, and packaged it for different operating systems. Whether you're building a small utility or a large-scale application, Electron makes it easy to leverage your web development skills to create powerful desktop applications.

Now that you know the core concepts, you can start building more advanced desktop applications. Experiment with adding features like notifications, file handling, and even integration with web services to enhance your apps. The possibilities are endless!

Chapter 6: Integrating React Native and Electron

Building cross-platform applications allows you to reach users on multiple devices and platforms, ensuring that your app has the widest reach and usability. With **React Native** for mobile apps and **Electron** for desktop apps, you have powerful tools at your disposal. But what if you could combine both to create a truly integrated experience across devices? In this chapter, we will explore how to bring **React Native** and **Electron** together into a unified, seamless experience that works on both mobile and desktop. We'll walk you through building a **Cross-Platform File Manager**, syncing data between platforms, ensuring a consistent user interface (UI), and testing across different devices.

Bringing Mobile and Desktop Together

The goal of building cross-platform apps is to provide users with a consistent, seamless experience, regardless of the device they are using. By integrating **React Native** and **Electron**, you can achieve this by creating an app that works both on mobile and desktop platforms while maintaining the same look, feel, and functionality.

How React Native and Electron Work Together

Before we dive into the project, let's briefly discuss how **React Native** and **Electron** can be integrated:

- **React Native** is primarily used for building mobile applications for iOS and Android.

It uses a single JavaScript codebase to create mobile apps that have native performance and look-and-feel.

- **Electron** is used for building desktop applications using web technologies like HTML, CSS, and JavaScript, which are wrapped in a Chromium browser window and packaged into a native desktop app for macOS, Windows, and Linux.

Both frameworks rely on JavaScript, and through their shared ecosystem, it's easy to ensure that your logic and some codebase can be reused across platforms. The key to a smooth integration is making sure that the app's **UI and data flow** are consistent across devices.

Example: Imagine a file manager app that allows users to view, edit, and organize their files both on their mobile device and desktop. The app will feature:

- A similar user interface on both platforms (e.g., list of files, buttons to add or remove files).

- Synchronization of files across devices.

Project: Building a Cross-Platform File Manager

Let's dive into creating a cross-platform **file manager app** that will work on both mobile and desktop. This will be a simple app where users can:

- View files and folders.

- Add and remove files.

- Sync data between mobile and desktop devices.

We'll break the project into manageable steps:

Step 1: Setting Up Your Project

1. **Create a New Directory for the Project**: Let's start by creating a directory for your project. This will contain both the React Native and Electron parts of your app.

bash

```
mkdir cross-platform-file-manager
cd cross-platform-file-manager
```

2. **Set Up React Native**: Initialize a new **React Native** project inside the cross-platform-file-manager directory.

bash

```
npx react-native init
FileManagerMobile
cd FileManagerMobile
```

3. **Set Up Electron**: Now, go back to the root directory (cross-platform-file-manager) and

set up **Electron**. Create a new directory for Electron:

bash

```
mkdir electron-app
cd electron-app
npm init -y
npm install electron --save-dev
```

4. **Folder Structure**: The project structure should look like this:

bash

```
/cross-platform-file-manager
  /FileManagerMobile (React Native
app)
  /electron-app (Electron app)
```

Step 2: Building the User Interface (UI)

Now that we have the project structure, let's focus on the UI. We want the mobile and desktop UI to have a consistent layout. Here's how we can build that.

1. **React Native UI**: We'll start by building the UI for the mobile app (React Native). Open FileManagerMobile/App.js and add the following basic layout:

```javascript

import React, { useState } from
'react';
import { View, Text, Button,
FlatList, StyleSheet } from
'react-native';

const App = () => {
```

```
const [files, setFiles] =
useState(['file1.txt',
'file2.txt', 'file3.txt']);

const handleAddFile = () => {
  const newFile =
`file${files.length + 1}.txt`;
  setFiles([...files, newFile]);
};

return (
  <View
style={styles.container}>
    <Text
style={styles.header}>File
Manager</Text>
    <Button title="Add File"
onPress={handleAddFile} />
    <FlatList
      data={files}
```

```
        keyExtractor={(item) =>
item}
        renderItem={({ item }) =>
<Text
style={styles.file}>{item}</Text>}
      />
    </View>
  );
};


const styles = StyleSheet.create({
  container: {
    flex: 1,
    justifyContent: 'center',
    alignItems: 'center',
    padding: 20,
    backgroundColor: '#f0f0f0',
  },
  header: {
    fontSize: 24,
    marginBottom: 20,
```

```
  },
  file: {
    fontSize: 18,
    padding: 10,
  },
});
```

```
export default App;
```

This simple UI has:

- o A header with the title "File Manager".

- o A button to add files.

- o A FlatList to display the list of files.

2. **Electron UI**: Next, let's create a similar UI for the desktop version using **Electron**. Create a file called electron-app/index.html with the following content:

```
html
```

```html
<!DOCTYPE html>
<html lang="en">
<head>
  <meta charset="UTF-8" />
  <meta name="viewport"
content="width=device-width,
initial-scale=1.0" />
  <title>File Manager</title>
  <style>
    body {
      font-family: Arial, sans-
serif;
      display: flex;
      flex-direction: column;
      justify-content: center;
      align-items: center;
      background-color: #f0f0f0;
      height: 100vh;
      margin: 0;
    }
    button {
```

```
      padding: 10px 20px;
      font-size: 16px;
      margin: 10px;
    }
    ul {
      list-style-type: none;
      padding: 0;
    }
    li {
      font-size: 18px;
      padding: 10px;
    }
  </style>
</head>
<body>
  <h1>File Manager</h1>
  <button id="addFileBtn">Add
File</button>
  <ul id="fileList"></ul>
```

```
  <script
src="renderer.js"></script>
</body>
</html>
```

In the index.html file:

- The layout is similar to the React Native version.

- We have an **Add File** button and an unordered list (ul) to display files.

3. **Renderer Process (Electron)**: Now, let's add functionality to the Electron UI. Create a file called renderer.js inside the electron-app folder with the following code:

javascript

```
const addFileButton =
document.getElementById('addFileBt
n');
```

```javascript
const fileList =
document.getElementById('fileList'
);

let files = ['file1.txt',
'file2.txt', 'file3.txt'];

const updateFileList = () => {
  fileList.innerHTML = '';
  files.forEach((file) => {
    const li =
document.createElement('li');
    li.textContent = file;
    fileList.appendChild(li);
  });
};

addFileButton.addEventListener('cl
ick', () => {
  const newFile =
`file${files.length + 1}.txt`;
```

```
files.push(newFile);
updateFileList();
});
```

```
updateFileList();
```

This JavaScript file:

- o Handles the **Add File** button click event to add a new file to the list.

- o Updates the fileList to display the files.

Step 3: Syncing Data Between Platforms

Now that we have the basic UI in place for both the mobile and desktop versions of the file manager, let's focus on syncing data between the platforms. We can achieve this using **local storage** or an **API** to persist the files. For this example, we'll use **local storage**.

- **Mobile App Sync:** In the React Native app, we'll use **AsyncStorage** to save the list of files locally.

- **Desktop App Sync:** In the Electron app, we'll use **Node.js fs module** to save the list of files in a local text file.

This way, both apps will have their own local storage, but when data is added or changed, it will sync by reading from the local storage and updating the UI accordingly.

Testing Across Platforms

Testing is crucial when developing cross-platform applications. You need to ensure that your app functions correctly on different devices (mobile and desktop) and that the user experience is consistent.

Testing React Native App

1. **Use Emulators and Simulators**: Test the mobile app on **iOS** and **Android** emulators. Use **Xcode** for iOS and **Android Studio** for Android. Emulators allow you to simulate different device screen sizes and test responsiveness.

2. **Manual Testing**: Test all functionalities manually, such as adding, editing, and removing files, to ensure everything works as expected.

3. **Automated Testing**: Use testing frameworks like **Jest** or **Detox** for end-to-end testing of the mobile app. Detox allows you to automate testing on mobile devices

by interacting with the app's UI programmatically.

Testing Electron App

1. **Test on Different OS**: Electron allows you to build apps for **Windows, macOS**, and **Linux**. Test your app on all three platforms to ensure compatibility. You can use virtual machines or multiple devices to do this.

2. **Test with Different Screen Resolutions**: Make sure your app's UI adjusts properly across different screen sizes. Electron apps should be responsive to ensure a smooth user experience across various desktop devices.

3. **Automated Testing**: Use tools like **Spectron** (for Electron) to automate end-to-end tests for your desktop application. Spectron can interact with Electron apps in

a similar way to how Selenium interacts with web apps.

Conclusion

In this chapter, we've explored how to integrate **React Native** and **Electron** to create a cross-platform file manager app. By leveraging the strengths of both frameworks, we built a consistent UI, synced data across mobile and desktop platforms, and ensured the app worked seamlessly on both. Additionally, we covered testing strategies to ensure that your app functions properly across different devices and platforms.

With this foundation, you can expand your knowledge and build more complex, integrated applications that run smoothly on mobile and desktop. Keep experimenting, and soon you'll be creating fully integrated apps that users love!

Chapter 7: Mastering Data Synchronization

In the modern world of mobile and desktop applications, data synchronization is a critical aspect of app development. Ensuring that data is consistent across multiple platforms—whether on mobile, desktop, or server—is a fundamental challenge. This chapter will dive into the intricacies of data synchronization, discuss the best practices and strategies for handling it, and guide you through building a **sync-enabled notes app** that works seamlessly across **React Native, Electron**, and **Node.js**. Additionally, we'll cover how to implement **offline functionality** so your app continues to function even when there's no active internet connection, with automatic data syncing once the connection is restored.

The Importance of Syncing Data Across Platforms

Data synchronization refers to the process of ensuring that information is consistently updated and stored across multiple devices or platforms. Whether you're working with **mobile**, **desktop**, or **server-side** applications, syncing data ensures that users have a seamless experience across all their devices. Without proper synchronization, users might face issues like losing data when switching devices, outdated content, or conflicting changes.

Challenges of Data Synchronization

Syncing data between multiple platforms can present several challenges:

- **Conflict Resolution**: When the same data is modified on multiple devices, you need a mechanism to resolve conflicts. Without this, changes from one platform could overwrite or interfere with changes made on another.

- **Latency**: If your app relies on a server for syncing data, network latency can affect how quickly the data is updated across platforms.

- **Offline Scenarios**: Users may not always have access to the internet, but the app must still function and store data locally. Once the connection is restored, the app should sync data correctly.

- **Data Storage and Security**: Ensuring data is securely stored and synced without compromising performance or user privacy is vital.

Best Practices for Data Synchronization

To address these challenges and create an efficient and reliable synchronization system, consider the following best practices:

1. **Use Local Storage for Temporary Data**: Use local storage to temporarily hold data when a user is offline. This allows the app to function even when there's no internet connection.

2. **Implement Conflict-Free Data Structures**: Implement data structures and systems (e.g., CRDTs—Conflict-free Replicated Data Types) that minimize conflicts and ensure that changes are merged without losing data.

3. **Asynchronous Synchronization**: Sync data asynchronously in the background to

prevent blocking the app's main process and to enhance the user experience.

4. **Sync on Reconnect**: Ensure the app can detect when a connection is re-established and automatically sync the data with the server or other devices.

5. **Data Encryption**: Always encrypt sensitive data during synchronization to protect users' privacy and ensure secure data transmission.

Project: Building a Sync-Enabled Notes App

In this project, we'll create a **Notes app** that works across multiple platforms (React Native for mobile and Electron for desktop), and syncs data in real-time using **Node.js** as the backend. The app will allow users to take notes, and all changes will be reflected on every device that the user has logged into.

Step 1: Setting Up the Project

We'll start by setting up a new directory for the project, creating the necessary files for both the **React Native mobile app** and the **Electron desktop app**, and setting up **Node.js** to serve as the backend.

1. **Create the Project Directory:** Let's create a folder for your project and initialize the necessary parts.

bash

```
mkdir notes-sync-app
cd notes-sync-app
```

2. **Set Up React Native (Mobile App):** Create a new React Native project using the following command:

```bash
```

```bash
npx react-native init NotesMobile
cd NotesMobile
```

3. **Set Up Electron (Desktop App)**: Go back to the root directory and create the Electron app directory:

```bash
```

```bash
mkdir electron-app
cd electron-app
npm init -y
npm install electron --save-dev
```

4. **Set Up Node.js Backend**: Go back to the root directory and initialize a simple **Node.js backend**:

```bash
```

```bash
mkdir node-backend
cd node-backend
```

```
npm init -y
npm install express mongoose
```

Step 2: Designing the Notes App UI

Let's focus on creating a consistent UI that works across both mobile and desktop platforms. We'll use basic components in **React Native** and **HTML** for Electron.

1. **React Native UI (Mobile App):** Open the App.js file in the React Native project and create the basic UI for the Notes app.

javascript

```javascript
import React, { useState,
useEffect } from 'react';
import { View, TextInput, Button,
FlatList, Text, StyleSheet } from
'react-native';
import axios from 'axios';
```

```
const App = () => {
  const [note, setNote] =
useState('');
  const [notes, setNotes] =
useState([]);

  // Fetch notes from the server
  const fetchNotes = async () => {
    try {
      const response = await
axios.get('http://localhost:5000/n
otes');
      setNotes(response.data);
    } catch (error) {
      console.error('Error
fetching notes:', error);
    }
  };

  useEffect(() => {
```

```
    fetchNotes();
  }, []);


  // Add note to the server
  const addNote = async () => {
    try {
      await
axios.post('http://localhost:5000/
notes', { content: note });
      setNote('');
      fetchNotes();
    } catch (error) {
      console.error('Error adding
note:', error);
    }
  };


  return (
    <View
style={styles.container}>
      <TextInput
```

```
        style={styles.input}
        placeholder="Write a note"
        value={note}
        onChangeText={setNote}
      />
      <Button title="Add Note"
onPress={addNote} />
      <FlatList
        data={notes}
        keyExtractor={(item) =>
item._id}
        renderItem={({ item }) =>
<Text>{item.content}</Text>}
      />
    </View>
  );
};

const styles = StyleSheet.create({
  container: {
    flex: 1,
```

```
    padding: 20,
  },
  input: {
    height: 40,
    borderColor: 'gray',
    borderWidth: 1,
    marginBottom: 10,
    paddingLeft: 10,
  },
});
```

```
export default App;
```

2. **Electron UI (Desktop App)**: Next, create a simple UI for the desktop version. Create an index.html file inside the electron-app folder with the following content:

```
html
```

```html
<!DOCTYPE html>
<html lang="en">
```

```html
<head>
  <meta charset="UTF-8">
  <meta name="viewport"
content="width=device-width,
initial-scale=1.0">
  <title>Notes App</title>
</head>
<body>
  <h1>Notes App</h1>
  <input type="text"
id="noteInput" placeholder="Write
a note" />
  <button id="addNoteBtn">Add
Note</button>
  <ul id="notesList"></ul>

  <script
src="renderer.js"></script>
</body>
</html>
```

3. **Handling Data in the Electron App (renderer.js):** Next, create the renderer.js file in the electron-app folder. This will handle the interaction for the desktop app, allowing users to add notes and view them.

```javascript
const addNoteBtn =
document.getElementById('addNoteBt
n');
const noteInput =
document.getElementById('noteInput
');
const notesList =
document.getElementById('notesList
');

const fetchNotes = async () => {
  try {
```

```
    const response = await
fetch('http://localhost:5000/notes
');
    const notes = await
response.json();
    notesList.innerHTML =
notes.map(note =>
`<li>${note.content}</li>`).join('
');
  } catch (error) {
    console.error('Error fetching
notes:', error);
  }
};

addNoteBtn.addEventListener('click
', async () => {
  const noteContent =
noteInput.value;
  try {
```

```
    await
fetch('http://localhost:5000/notes
', {
      method: 'POST',
      headers: { 'Content-Type':
'application/json' },
      body: JSON.stringify({
content: noteContent }),
    });
    noteInput.value = '';
    fetchNotes();
  } catch (error) {
    console.error('Error adding
note:', error);
  }
});

fetchNotes();
```

Step 3: Backend Implementation with Node.js

Now, let's set up the **Node.js backend** that will handle storing and retrieving notes.

1. **Backend Setup (server.js):** Inside the node-backend folder, create a server.js file to define the Express API and MongoDB connection:

javascript

```javascript
const express =
require('express');
const mongoose =
require('mongoose');
const cors = require('cors');
const bodyParser = require('body-
parser');

const app = express();
```

```
app.use(cors());
app.use(bodyParser.json());

mongoose.connect('mongodb://localh
ost:27017/notesApp', {
  useNewUrlParser: true,
  useUnifiedTopology: true,
});

const noteSchema = new
mongoose.Schema({
  content: String,
});

const Note =
mongoose.model('Note',
noteSchema);

app.get('/notes', async (req, res)
=> {
  const notes = await Note.find();
```

```
  res.json(notes);
});


app.post('/notes', async (req,
res) => {
  const { content } = req.body;
  const note = new Note({ content
});
  await note.save();
  res.status(201).send(note);
});


const PORT = 5000;
app.listen(PORT, () => {
  console.log(`Server running on
port ${PORT}`);
});
```

This backend:

- Handles **GET** requests to fetch all notes.

o Handles **POST** requests to add new notes to the database.

Offline Functionality

One of the essential features for modern apps is **offline functionality**. This allows users to continue using the app even without an active internet connection, and sync data when the connection is restored.

Implementing Offline Mode in the Notes App

1. **Mobile (React Native) Offline Mode**: To implement offline functionality in the React Native app, we'll use **AsyncStorage** to store notes locally when the device is offline. Once the device is online again, the app will sync the notes with the server.

First, install AsyncStorage:

```bash

npm install @react-native-async-storage/async-storage
```

Then, modify the app to store notes locally when offline and sync them later.

2. **Desktop (Electron) Offline Mode**: In Electron, you can use **localStorage** or a more robust storage solution like **NeDB** to store data locally. When the app is online again, it can sync with the backend to update the server.

Conclusion

In this chapter, you learned how to implement **data synchronization** across mobile and desktop applications using **React Native**, **Electron**, and

Node.js. We built a simple **Notes app** that syncs data in real-time, ensuring consistency across platforms. Additionally, we implemented **offline functionality**, allowing the app to continue working even when the user is not connected to the internet, and syncing once the connection is restored.

Mastering data synchronization is crucial for building seamless, efficient applications, and with the tools and techniques covered in this chapter, you now have the foundation to build robust, cross-platform apps that users can rely on. Keep experimenting and building, and soon you'll be able to create even more powerful apps!

Chapter 8: Optimizing Performance

In this chapter, we will explore various strategies and best practices for optimizing the performance of mobile, server-side, and desktop applications. Whether you are working with **React Native**, **Node.js**, or **Electron**, each platform comes with its own set of challenges when it comes to performance. However, by implementing the right strategies, you can make your apps faster, more responsive, and scalable. We will discuss techniques for reducing render times, handling complex animations, managing memory efficiently, and making sure your app delivers an exceptional user experience across all devices.

React Native Performance Best Practices

Performance optimization in React Native is critical for ensuring a smooth and responsive user experience. While React Native provides great flexibility, developers need to pay attention to specific areas like render times, memory usage, and animations. Let's break down how you can tackle these challenges and make your React Native app perform at its best.

1. Reducing Render Times

Render times in React Native are often impacted by the number of components being rendered and the complexity of those components. When you are building an app with many UI elements, it's essential to reduce the render times for each component to avoid lag and improve performance.

Use React.memo for Component Optimization

React provides React.memo, a higher-order component that can help prevent unnecessary re-renders by memoizing components. When props haven't changed, React skips the re-render, improving performance.

Example:

```javascript
const ListItem = React.memo(({
title }) => {
  return <Text>{title}</Text>;
});
```

In this example, if the title prop does not change, React will not re-render the ListItem component.

Optimize FlatList Performance

FlatList is a powerful component for rendering large lists in React Native. However, it can also become a performance bottleneck if not used properly. To optimize its performance:

- Use keyExtractor to uniquely identify each item in the list.

- Use initialNumToRender to limit the number of items that render initially.

- Enable getItemLayout for a flat list when the item size is fixed.

Example:

```javascript

<FlatList
  data={data}
  keyExtractor={(item) =>
item.id.toString()}
  initialNumToRender={10}
```

```
getItemLayout={(data, index) =>
(
    { length: 50, offset: 50 *
index, index }
  )}
  renderItem={({ item }) =>
<ListItem title={item.title} />}
/>
```

This ensures that only a minimal number of items are rendered initially, and the list will be more efficient as the user scrolls.

---

2. Handling Complex Animations

Complex animations can sometimes lead to performance issues in React Native, especially when dealing with large, intricate movements or transitions. By leveraging the right tools, you can ensure that animations remain smooth and efficient.

Use React Native Reanimated

For complex animations, **React Native Reanimated** is a more efficient alternative to the built-in **Animated API**. Reanimated allows for animations to run on the native thread, bypassing the JavaScript thread and improving performance.

Example of a simple animation with React Native Reanimated:

```javascript
import Animated, { Easing } from
'react-native-reanimated';

const translateX = new
Animated.Value(0);

const startAnimation = () => {
  Animated.timing(translateX, {
```

```
    toValue: 100,
    duration: 500,
    easing: Easing.ease,
  }).start();
};


return (
  <Animated.View style={{
transform: [{ translateX }] }} />
);
```

Reanimated allows for complex animations while offloading processing to the native thread, avoiding performance bottlenecks.

Avoid Blocking the Main Thread

Ensure that heavy computations and animations are not blocking the main thread. If a complex calculation or animation is blocking the UI thread, it can cause performance issues like janky frames or UI lag. Offload complex tasks to the background using asynchronous operations such as setTimeout, setInterval, or requestIdleCallback to avoid blocking the UI.

---

3. Minimizing Memory Usage

Memory management is key to optimizing React Native app performance. Poor memory usage can lead to slowdowns, crashes, and unresponsiveness, especially on lower-end devices.

Profile and Identify Memory Leaks

React Native provides built-in tools to profile memory usage and detect potential memory leaks. Use the **React Developer Tools** and **Flipper** for inspecting your app's memory usage. Regularly check if objects are properly disposed of and cleaned up when no longer needed.

You can also use **useEffect** hooks to clean up resources like event listeners or network requests:

```javascript

useEffect(() => {
  const fetchData = () => {
    // Fetching logic
  };


  fetchData();


  return () => {
    // Cleanup logic, like
aborting fetch requests
  };
}, []);
```

Improving Node.js Performance

Node.js is a powerful backend technology that allows you to build scalable applications. However, performance optimization is crucial when your application handles large numbers of requests, processes heavy computations, or deals with complex data.

1. Handling Concurrency in Node.js

Node.js operates on a single-threaded event loop, which is highly efficient for I/O-heavy tasks. However, to achieve true concurrency (parallel processing), you need to use worker threads or asynchronous programming.

Use Worker Threads for Parallelism

Node.js introduced **Worker Threads** in version 10.5.0 to help you perform CPU-intensive tasks in parallel, without blocking the event loop.

Example:

javascript

```
const { Worker, isMainThread,
parentPort } =
require('worker_threads');

if (isMainThread) {
   const worker = new
Worker(__filename);

   worker.on('message', (result) =>
{
      console.log(result); //
Process the result from the worker
   });

   worker.postMessage('start'); //
Send a message to the worker
} else {
   parentPort.on('message',
(message) => {
      // Perform CPU-intensive task
here
```

```
    parentPort.postMessage('Task
complete');
    });
}
```

In this example, the heavy computation is offloaded to the worker thread, ensuring that the main thread remains unblocked.

2. Optimizing Database Queries

Slow database queries can significantly impact the performance of your Node.js application. Here are some strategies to improve database performance:

Use Indexing

Indexes help speed up query execution by reducing the amount of data that the database needs to scan. Ensure that commonly queried fields (like user IDs or timestamps) are indexed in your database.

Limit and Paginate Results

When querying large datasets, always paginate the results to avoid overloading your server with too much data at once. Use limit and skip in MongoDB queries or OFFSET and LIMIT in SQL queries.

Example:

```javascript
```

```
// MongoDB
db.collection('notes').find().limi
t(10).skip(20);
```

This will return 10 notes starting from the 20th record, ensuring that the data returned is manageable.

Use Caching

Caching frequently accessed data can greatly improve response times and reduce the load on your database. Use tools like **Redis** to cache data in memory.

Example of using Redis in Node.js:

```javascript
const redis = require('redis');
const client =
redis.createClient();

client.set('notes',
JSON.stringify(notes));
client.get('notes', (err, data) =>
{
    if (err) throw err;
    const notes = JSON.parse(data);
    console.log(notes);
});
```

By caching the results of frequently queried data, you can reduce the number of requests made to the database and improve your application's response time.

---

3. Optimizing Node.js Middleware

Middleware functions in Node.js are often responsible for handling requests before they are passed to the actual route handlers. By optimizing middleware, you can improve the overall performance of your Node.js application.

Use Efficient Middleware

- Avoid using too many middleware layers that perform heavy processing.

- Place lightweight middleware (like logging) early in the chain, while more complex ones (like authentication) can come later.

- Use **compression** middleware to compress response data and reduce payload size.

Example of using compression:

```
javascript


const compression =
require('compression');
app.use(compression());
```

This reduces the size of the response body, improving data transfer speeds.

Boosting Electron App Efficiency

Electron applications can sometimes become sluggish if not optimized correctly. Because Electron wraps web technologies inside a native container, performance can degrade if the app is not well-optimized. Below are strategies to ensure your Electron app performs efficiently.

1. Lazy Loading for Electron

One way to improve performance is to implement **lazy loading,** which delays the loading of resources or components until they are needed.

Lazy Load Routes

Electron uses a main process to manage app windows and renderer processes to render the UI. You can lazy-load certain routes or modules in the renderer process to minimize the initial load time of the app.

Example:

```javascript

const React = lazy(() =>
import('./MyComponent'));
```

In this example, MyComponent will only be loaded when required, rather than loading all components upfront.

2. Reducing App Size

The size of Electron apps can grow quickly due to bundled dependencies. To reduce the size of your app, consider the following approaches:

- Use **electron-builder** to package your app efficiently.

- Remove unused libraries and assets that are not critical to your app's functionality.

- Use **native modules** when possible, instead of bundling large web dependencies.

Electron-builder Example for Optimized Packaging

You can use **electron-builder** to package and distribute your app in a way that minimizes its size:

```bash
```

```bash
npm install electron-builder --save-dev
```

Then, define the build configuration in your package.json:

```json
```

```json
"build": {
  "appId": "com.example.desktop",
  "productName": "DesktopApp",
  "files": [
    "**/*"
  ]
}
```

Run electron-builder to package the app:

```bash
```

```
npm run dist
```

3. Improving Startup Performance

Electron apps can sometimes have long startup times due to the resources loaded during the initial launch. To improve this:

- Defer the loading of heavy resources.

- Minimize the number of processes spawned at startup.

- Use **webpack** for bundling the renderer process to reduce file sizes and improve startup time.

Optimizing Startup

You can optimize the startup by not loading unnecessary content during the initial launch, and instead load critical resources first.

```javascript
```

```
app.on('ready', () => {
  createWindow();
  setImmediate(() =>
loadOtherResources());
});
```

This ensures that only the essential resources are loaded first, allowing the app to become usable more quickly.

Conclusion

Optimizing the performance of your apps—whether they are built with React Native, Node.js, or Electron—is crucial for delivering a seamless user experience. By following the best practices discussed in this chapter:

- You can improve **React Native** performance by reducing render times, handling animations efficiently, and minimizing memory usage.

- You can enhance the **Node.js** backend performance by handling concurrency, optimizing database queries, and implementing caching strategies.

- You can boost **Electron** app efficiency by using lazy loading, reducing app size, and improving startup performance.

As you continue building apps, always focus on performance optimization to ensure that your applications not only function well but also provide the best possible experience for your users. Keep experimenting with these strategies, and your apps will run smoother, faster, and more efficiently across platforms!

Chapter 9: Security and Authentication

In the world of software development, security is one of the most important aspects to consider. Whether you're building a mobile app, a web application, or a desktop app, securing your application is crucial for protecting sensitive data, preventing unauthorized access, and ensuring a seamless user experience. This chapter will cover essential aspects of security for cross-platform applications, including how to protect against common vulnerabilities such as SQL injection, Cross-Site Scripting (XSS), and Cross-Site Request Forgery (CSRF). We will also walk through a project on implementing **user authentication** using **OAuth** or **JWT (JSON Web Tokens)** and explore best practices for **encryption** and **secure data storage**.

Securing Cross-Platform Applications

Cross-platform applications need robust security measures to prevent various attacks that target both the client-side and server-side of your app. In this section, we will explore some of the most common vulnerabilities in web and mobile apps and how to mitigate them.

1. SQL Injection

SQL Injection occurs when an attacker is able to inject malicious SQL code into a query, potentially allowing them to manipulate the database. This can lead to unauthorized access, data corruption, or even full control over the database.

Preventing SQL Injection

To prevent SQL Injection:

- **Use Prepared Statements**: Always use prepared statements or parameterized queries when interacting with the database. This ensures that user input is treated as data, not executable code.

Example using Node.js with MySQL:

```javascript
const mysql = require('mysql');
```

```
const db =
mysql.createConnection({ /*
connection details */ });

const userQuery = 'SELECT * FROM
users WHERE username = ?';
db.query(userQuery, [username],
(err, results) => {
  if (err) throw err;
  // process results
});
```

In this example, the ? is a placeholder, and the actual username will be safely inserted by the database driver, preventing malicious code injection.

- **Sanitize Input**: Always sanitize user input, especially when dealing with string values like email addresses or search terms. Libraries like **validator** or **sanitize-html** can help sanitize input before it's used in database queries.

---

2. Cross-Site Scripting (XSS)

Cross-Site Scripting (XSS) occurs when an attacker injects malicious scripts (typically JavaScript) into a web page that is viewed by other users. These scripts can be used to steal cookies, capture keystrokes, or perform other malicious actions.

Preventing XSS Attacks

To prevent XSS:

- **Escape Output:** Ensure that user-generated content is properly escaped when rendered in the browser. This will prevent any embedded scripts from being executed.

- **Use Content Security Policy (CSP)**: A **CSP** is a security feature that helps detect and mitigate certain types of attacks, including XSS. It restricts the sources from which content can be loaded.

Example of escaping HTML with React:

```javascript
const SafeComponent = ({ text })
=> {
  const safeText =
text.replace(/</g,
"&lt;").replace(/>/g, "&gt;");
  return <div>{safeText}</div>;
};
```

In React, using dangerouslySetInnerHTML can lead to XSS vulnerabilities. Always sanitize or escape HTML content before injecting it into the DOM.

- **Sanitize Input Fields**: For form fields where users can input HTML (like a rich text editor), sanitize input using libraries like **DOMPurify**.

---

3. Cross-Site Request Forgery (CSRF)

Cross-Site Request Forgery (CSRF) is an attack where a user is tricked into executing unwanted actions on a website where they are authenticated. This can be particularly dangerous if a user's session is hijacked.

Preventing CSRF

To prevent CSRF:

- **Use Anti-CSRF Tokens**: One of the most effective ways to prevent CSRF is to generate a unique, secret token for each request that modifies data. This token is sent along with the request and validated on the server to ensure the request is legitimate.

Example with Express.js (Node.js):

javascript

```
const csrf = require('csurf');
const csrfProtection = csrf({ cookie: true });


app.post('/update-profile', csrfProtection, (req, res) => {
  // process form submission
});
```

In this example, the csrfProtection middleware ensures that every POST request contains a valid CSRF token.

- **SameSite Cookies**: Use the SameSite cookie attribute to prevent cookies from being sent in cross-site requests, which can help mitigate CSRF attacks.

```javascript
cookie: { sameSite: 'Strict' }
```

Project: Implementing User Authentication

User authentication is a critical part of securing an app. In this section, we will implement a basic authentication system using **JWT (JSON Web Tokens)** or **OAuth** for secure user login.

1. What is Authentication?

Authentication is the process of verifying the identity of a user. In web applications, this often involves the user providing a username and password, which is then checked against a stored database. If the credentials match, the user is authenticated.

2. Using JWT for User Authentication

JSON Web Tokens (JWT) are a popular method for handling user authentication in modern web applications. JWT is a compact, URL-safe token format that is used to securely transmit information between the client and server.

Setting Up JWT Authentication with Node.js

Let's set up a simple authentication system using JWT in Node.js. We will use **Express** and **jsonwebtoken** to issue and verify tokens.

1. **Install Dependencies:**

```bash
```

```
npm install express jsonwebtoken
bcryptjs
```

2. Create the Authentication Route:

In your Node.js backend (server.js), create a route to handle user login and generate a JWT token.

```javascript

const express =
require('express');
const bcrypt =
require('bcryptjs');
const jwt =
require('jsonwebtoken');
const app = express();
const users = []; // This should
be a database in production

app.use(express.json());
```

```
// Register user
app.post('/register', (req, res)
=> {
  const { username, password } =
req.body;
  const hashedPassword =
bcrypt.hashSync(password, 8);
  users.push({ username, password:
hashedPassword });
  res.status(201).send('User
registered');
});

// Login user
app.post('/login', (req, res) => {
  const { username, password } =
req.body;
  const user = users.find(u =>
u.username === username);
```

```
  if (!user) return
res.status(404).send('User not
found');

  const passwordIsValid =
bcrypt.compareSync(password,
user.password);
  if (!passwordIsValid) return
res.status(401).send('Invalid
password');

  const token = jwt.sign({ id:
user.username }, 'your-secret-
key', { expiresIn: '1h' });
  res.status(200).json({ token });
});

// Middleware to verify JWT token
const verifyToken = (req, res,
next) => {
```

```
const token = req.headers['x-
access-token'];
 if (!token) return
res.status(403).send('No token
provided');


 jwt.verify(token, 'your-secret-
key', (err, decoded) => {
  if (err) return
res.status(500).send('Failed to
authenticate token');
   req.userId = decoded.id;
   next();
 });
};


app.get('/protected', verifyToken,
(req, res) => {
 res.status(200).send('This is a
protected route');
});
```

```
app.listen(5000, () => {
  console.log('Server running on
port 5000');
});
```

- **Register:** The /register route hashes the user's password and stores it in the users array.

- **Login:** The /login route checks if the user exists, compares the password, and issues a JWT token if authentication is successful.

- **JWT Verification:** The verifyToken middleware verifies the token before accessing protected routes.

3. Using OAuth for User Authentication

OAuth is an open standard for authorization. Unlike JWT, which is mainly used for authentication, OAuth allows third-party applications to access user data without exposing credentials.

Setting Up OAuth with Node.js

To use OAuth, you typically integrate with a service provider (such as Google, Facebook, or GitHub) for authentication.

1. **Install Passport.js and OAuth Strategies:**

```bash
bash
```

```
npm install passport passport-google-oauth20 express-session
```

2. **OAuth Authentication with Google:**

Here's how to implement Google authentication using **Passport.js** and **OAuth2.0**.

```javascript
const passport =
require('passport');
const GoogleStrategy =
require('passport-google-
oauth20').Strategy;
const express =
require('express');
const session = require('express-
session');
const app = express();

passport.use(new GoogleStrategy({
    clientID:
'YOUR_GOOGLE_CLIENT_ID',
    clientSecret:
'YOUR_GOOGLE_CLIENT_SECRET',
```

```
    callbackURL:
'http://localhost:5000/auth/google
/callback',
  },
  (accessToken, refreshToken,
profile, done) => {
    return done(null, profile);
  }
));

app.use(session({ secret: 'your-
secret', resave: false,
saveUninitialized: true }));
app.use(passport.initialize());
app.use(passport.session());

app.get('/auth/google',
  passport.authenticate('google',
{ scope: ['profile', 'email'] })
);
```

```
app.get('/auth/google/callback',
  passport.authenticate('google',
{ failureRedirect: '/' }),
  (req, res) => {
    res.redirect('/');
  }
);

app.get('/', (req, res) => {
  if (req.isAuthenticated()) {
    res.send(`<h1>Hello,
${req.user.displayName}</h1>`);
  } else {
    res.send('<a
href="/auth/google">Login with
Google</a>');
  }
});

app.listen(5000, () => {
```

```
console.log('Server running on
port 5000');
});
```

- **OAuth Authentication**: We use Passport.js with Google OAuth to authenticate users.

- **Session Management**: After successful authentication, the user's profile is saved in the session, allowing them to stay logged in.

Encryption and Secure Data Storage

Securing sensitive data, both on the client-side and server-side, is vital for protecting user privacy and preventing data breaches. In this section, we will explore best practices for encrypting data and securely storing it.

1. Encrypting Data on the Client-Side

When storing sensitive data (like passwords or API keys) on the client-side, it is essential to encrypt it before storage to prevent unauthorized access.

Client-Side Encryption with CryptoJS

You can use libraries like **CryptoJS** to encrypt and decrypt data in React Native or Electron apps.

Example using CryptoJS to encrypt a password:

bash

```
npm install crypto-js
```

javascript

```
import CryptoJS from 'crypto-js';
```

```
const encryptPassword = (password)
=> {
  const encryptedPassword =
CryptoJS.AES.encrypt(password,
'secret-key').toString();
  return encryptedPassword;
};

const decryptedPassword =
(encryptedPassword) => {
  const bytes =
CryptoJS.AES.decrypt(encryptedPass
word, 'secret-key');
  return
bytes.toString(CryptoJS.enc.Utf8);
};
```

In this example, we use **AES** encryption to securely encrypt and decrypt the password.

2. Encrypting Data on the Server-Side

On the server-side, encrypt sensitive data before storing it in a database. For example, encrypt passwords using **bcrypt** or **argon2** before saving them.

Using bcrypt to hash a password:

```bash
bash


npm install bcryptjs
javascript


const bcrypt =
require('bcryptjs');


// Hash password before saving to
database
const hashedPassword =
bcrypt.hashSync('password123', 8);
```

```
// Compare stored hash with input
const isMatch =
bcrypt.compareSync('password123',
hashedPassword);
```

In this example, bcrypt securely hashes passwords, preventing plain-text passwords from being stored in the database.

3. Secure Data Storage Best Practices

- **Use HTTPS**: Always use HTTPS to encrypt data in transit between the client and server.

- **Use Environment Variables for Secrets**: Never hardcode sensitive data (e.g., API keys, secrets) directly in your code. Use environment variables to store them securely.

- **Secure File Storage**: For sensitive files, store them in secure cloud storage providers that offer encryption at rest (e.g., Amazon S3 with encryption enabled).

Conclusion

In this chapter, we've covered the crucial aspects of **security and authentication** for cross-platform applications. From **securing against common vulnerabilities** like SQL Injection, XSS, and CSRF, to implementing **user authentication** using JWT or OAuth, and finally, ensuring **secure data storage** with encryption techniques, we've laid the foundation for building secure, reliable applications.

Security should always be a top priority when developing any application. By applying the concepts and best practices outlined here, you can ensure that your apps are robust, safe, and capable of protecting user data. As you continue developing, keep these security principles in mind to create applications that are both functional and secure.

Chapter 10: Deploying and Distributing Your Apps

Deploying and distributing your apps can often be the most challenging part of the development cycle. However, mastering the deployment process is essential to ensuring your app reaches its users and performs well in production. In this chapter, we will guide you through the process of deploying a **Node.js** backend to production, publishing **React Native** and **Electron** apps, and managing app versions and updates. By the end of this chapter, you'll have the knowledge and tools to get your app into the hands of users and keep it updated with ease.

Deploying Your Node.js Backend

Deploying your **Node.js** backend involves moving your application from your local development environment to a live server or cloud platform. You'll need to configure cloud services, set up automated deployment pipelines, and ensure that your app is properly monitored and secured.

[217]

1. Choosing a Cloud Platform

There are many cloud services available for deploying a **Node.js** backend, such as **Amazon Web Services (AWS)**, **Google Cloud Platform (GCP)**, **Microsoft Azure**, and **Heroku**. Each platform offers different features, but all are suitable for hosting a Node.js app. Let's explore deploying a Node.js app to **Heroku**, which is known for its simplicity and ease of use.

Setting Up Heroku

Heroku is a cloud platform that allows you to deploy, manage, and scale Node.js apps with minimal configuration. Here's how to deploy your Node.js backend to **Heroku**:

1. **Install the Heroku CLI**: First, you need to install the **Heroku CLI** (Command Line Interface) on your local machine. Visit the

Heroku website and follow the installation instructions for your operating system.

2. **Create a Heroku Account**: If you don't already have one, create a free account on Heroku's website.

3. **Prepare Your Node.js Application**: Your Node.js backend should have a Procfile to tell Heroku how to run your app. The Procfile is a simple text file that contains the following line:

```makefile
```

```
web: node server.js
```
This tells Heroku to use server.js as the entry point for the app.

4. **Deploying Your App**: Now, you're ready to deploy. Run the following commands:

```bash
```

```
git init
heroku create
git add .
git commit -m "Initial commit"
git push heroku master
```

After running these commands, Heroku will build and deploy your app. You can then visit your app by running:

```
bash
```

```
heroku open
```

5. **Environment Variables**: If your app uses environment variables (e.g., for API keys or database credentials), you can set them on Heroku using:

```
bash
```

```
heroku config:set
MY_API_KEY=yourapikey
```

6. **Scaling and Monitoring**: You can scale your app using the following command:

bash

```
heroku ps:scale web=1
```

You can also monitor your app's logs with:

bash

```
heroku logs --tail
```

By deploying to Heroku, your app is now live and ready to serve requests from users worldwide.

---

2. Setting Up Automated Deployment Pipelines

Automating the deployment process is essential for speeding up development and ensuring consistency. Many platforms, including **GitHub Actions**, **GitLab CI**, and **CircleCI**, allow you to automate deployment tasks such as building, testing, and deploying your app.

Example with GitHub Actions

GitHub Actions is an excellent tool for setting up continuous integration and continuous deployment (CI/CD) pipelines. Here's how to create a simple automated deployment pipeline for your Node.js app using GitHub Actions:

1. **Create a .github/workflows Directory**: In the root of your repository, create the .github/workflows directory.

2. **Create a Deployment Workflow File**: Inside the .github/workflows directory, create a file named deploy.yml with the following content:

```yaml
name: Node.js Deployment
```

```yaml
on:
  push:
    branches:
      - master

jobs:
  deploy:
    runs-on: ubuntu-latest

    steps:
    - name: Checkout code
      uses: actions/checkout@v2

    - name: Set up Node.js
      uses: actions/setup-node@v2
      with:
        node-version: '14'

    - name: Install dependencies
      run: npm install
```

```
  - name: Deploy to Heroku
    uses: akshnz/heroku-
action@v1
    with:
    heroku_api_key: ${{
secrets.HEROKU_API_KEY }}
      heroku_app_name: your-app-
name
      heroku_email: your-
email@example.com
```

This configuration automatically deploys the app to Heroku whenever you push changes to the master branch.

3. **Set Up Secrets**: In your GitHub repository settings, go to **Secrets** and add your **HEROKU_API_KEY**, heroku_app_name, and heroku_email as secrets.

4. **Push Changes**: Now, when you push to the master branch, GitHub Actions will automatically build and deploy your app to Heroku.

Publishing React Native and Electron Apps

Now that your backend is live, it's time to publish your mobile and desktop applications. This section will guide you through the process of publishing your **React Native** apps on **Google Play** and the **App Store**, as well as distributing **Electron** apps on various platforms.

1. Publishing React Native Apps

Publishing a React Native app involves creating an **APK** (Android) or **IPA** (iOS) file and submitting it to the respective stores.

Publishing to the Google Play Store

To publish an Android app to the Google Play Store, follow these steps:

1. **Generate a Signed APK**: You need to generate a signed APK file for your app. In the android directory of your React Native project, run:

bash

```
cd android
./gradlew assembleRelease
```

This will generate the APK in android/app/build/outputs/apk/release.

2. **Create a Google Play Developer Account**: Visit Google Play Console and create a developer account. There is a one-time fee of $25 to register.

3. **Upload Your APK**: After logging into the Google Play Console, click on **Create Application** and follow the prompts to upload your APK, fill out your app's details (description, screenshots, etc.), and submit it for review.

Publishing to the Apple App Store

Publishing to the App Store requires a bit more setup compared to Google Play. Follow these steps to publish your iOS app:

1. **Generate an IPA File**: In Xcode, open your React Native project and navigate to **Product > Archive** to create an archive of your app. Once archived, click **Distribute App** and select **App Store Connect**.

2. **Create an Apple Developer Account**: You'll need an **Apple Developer Program**

membership, which costs $99 per year. Register at Apple Developer Program.

3. **Upload the IPA to App Store Connect**: Once your IPA is ready, upload it to **App Store Connect** using Xcode or **Transporter**. After uploading, fill out your app's details and submit it for review.

2. Distributing Electron Apps

Electron apps can be distributed on **Windows, macOS**, and **Linux**. However, the distribution process differs slightly between platforms.

Distributing on Windows

1. **Use Electron-Builder**: Electron-builder simplifies the packaging and distribution of Electron apps. First, install electron-builder:

```bash
```

```
npm install electron-builder --
save-dev
```

2. **Configure Electron-Builder**: In your package.json file, configure the build settings for your app:

```json

"build": {
  "appId":
"com.example.electronapp",
  "productName": "ElectronApp",
  "win": {
    "target": "nsis"
  }
}
```

3. **Package the App**: Run the following command to package your app:

```bash

npm run dist
```

This will generate an installer .exe file that you can distribute.

Distributing on macOS

1. **Use Electron-Builder for macOS**: macOS distribution requires a valid Apple Developer account for signing the app. In package.json, configure the build settings for macOS:

```json
json

"build": {
  "mac": {
    "target": "dmg",
    "category": "public.app-
category.productivity"
  }
}
```

2. **Build and Sign the App**: Run the build command to create a .dmg file, and use **codesign** to sign the app for macOS:

```bash
```

```
npm run dist
```

Distributing on Linux

For Linux, you can create **deb** or **AppImage** files using **electron-builder**. The process is similar to that of macOS and Windows, but you will need to configure the Linux build targets in package.json and use the build command to package your app for Linux.

Managing App Versions and Updates

Managing app versions and ensuring smooth updates is critical for both user experience and maintaining security. This section discusses how to implement a version control system for your apps and how to push updates efficiently.

1. Version Control for Your Apps

Versioning ensures that your users are always using the latest version of the app. Proper version management allows you to keep track of changes, release new features, and fix bugs.

React Native Versioning

React Native uses **semantic versioning (semver)**, where version numbers follow the format MAJOR.MINOR.PATCH. When publishing a new version of your React Native app:

- Increment the **PATCH** version for bug fixes.

- Increment the **MINOR** version for new features.

- Increment the **MAJOR** version for breaking changes.

Electron Versioning

For Electron apps, you can use **electron-builder** to specify the app version in your package.json. Ensure that the version number is updated with each release:

```json
```

```json
"version": "1.0.0"
```

This ensures users receive the latest updates when they download or install the app.

---

2. Pushing App Updates

React Native Updates

To push updates to your React Native app, you can either submit a new version to the **App Store** or **Google Play** or use **over-the-air (OTA)** updates with **CodePush** (part of **App Center**). CodePush allows you to push updates directly to users without needing to go through the store review process.

Electron App Updates

For Electron apps, you can implement **auto-updating** using **electron-updater**. This allows your app to check for updates and install them automatically.

1. **Install electron-updater:**

bash

```
npm install electron-updater --save
```

2. **Enable Auto-Update:**

Add the following code in your Electron app to check for updates:

javascript

```
const { autoUpdater } =
require('electron-updater');

autoUpdater.checkForUpdatesAndNoti
fy();
```

This will ensure that users always have the latest version of your Electron app.

Conclusion

Deploying, distributing, and managing updates for your apps is a crucial part of the app development process. By following the steps in this chapter, you now have the knowledge to:

- Deploy your **Node.js** backend to the cloud with Heroku and set up automated deployment pipelines.

- Publish **React Native** apps to the Google Play Store and Apple App Store.

- Distribute **Electron** apps on Windows, macOS, and Linux platforms.

- Implement a version control system for your apps and push updates efficiently.

Now you are equipped to take your apps from development to production and ensure they remain up-to-date and secure for your users. The ability to manage app versions and streamline deployment is key to providing a seamless experience for your users. Keep experimenting and iterating on your apps, and soon you'll have a robust deployment process that works seamlessly across platforms.

Chapter 11: Real-World Application Case Studies

In this chapter, we're going to take a deep dive into **real-world cross-platform applications**. We'll explore some successful case studies of apps that have been built using **React Native, Electron**, and **Node.js**. By analyzing how these applications were built, you'll learn about the design choices, technologies, and best practices that make these apps successful.

After that, we'll walk through a **project-based learning exercise** where you'll build a more complex, real-world application like an **e-commerce** or **project management app** using the skills you've learned so far. Finally, we'll explore some of the **common challenges** developers face in cross-platform programming and share practical solutions to overcome them.

Analyzing Real-World Cross-Platform Apps

Many successful apps today are built using cross-platform technologies like **React Native**, **Electron**, and **Node.js**. These tools enable developers to write code once and deploy it across multiple platforms, saving both time and effort. Let's take a look at a few real-world examples of popular cross-platform apps, analyzing how they were developed and how they benefit from using these technologies.

1. Instagram (React Native)

Instagram is one of the most successful social media platforms in the world, with millions of active users. In 2016, Instagram made the decision to move its mobile app from a **native iOS/Android** codebase to **React Native**, a cross-platform framework. This decision allowed the team to focus on building features once and deploying them across both platforms.

How Instagram Uses React Native:

- **Shared Codebase**: By adopting React Native, Instagram was able to share a large portion of its codebase between iOS and Android, reducing the time and effort required to maintain separate native apps.

- **Real-Time Updates**: React Native allowed Instagram to deliver fast updates to both platforms simultaneously, improving the user experience and accelerating feature releases.

- **Performance Optimizations**: Instagram used **React Native's** ability to integrate native code where necessary, ensuring that performance was optimized for both platforms.

Lessons from Instagram's Use of React Native:

- **Evaluate the Need for Native Code**: Although React Native is powerful, there are still scenarios where using native code is necessary for performance or accessing platform-specific features. Instagram integrated native modules for parts of the app that required more customization or performance optimizations.

- **Consistent UI Across Platforms**: React Native enables developers to build consistent UIs across both iOS and Android, which is important for maintaining a unified brand experience.

2. Visual Studio Code (Electron)

Visual Studio Code (VSCode) is a widely used code editor developed by Microsoft. It's built using **Electron**, which allows the app to be written using web technologies like HTML, CSS, and JavaScript while maintaining the performance of a native application.

How VSCode Uses Electron:

- **Cross-Platform Support**: VSCode runs on **Windows, macOS**, and **Linux**, and using Electron enables the same codebase to work seamlessly across all these platforms.

- **Extension System**: VSCode's extension system allows users to install plugins that extend the functionality of the editor. Electron's ability to integrate web technologies makes it easy for developers to build and integrate extensions.

- **Performance**: Although Electron apps are known for being somewhat heavy, VSCode has optimized its app to provide a fast, responsive user experience, even with many extensions installed.

Lessons from VSCode's Use of Electron:

- **Optimization is Key**: While Electron allows for cross-platform development, performance optimization is crucial. VSCode makes use of various optimizations, such as **lazy loading**, to keep the app fast and responsive.

- **Modular Architecture**: The extension system is one of VSCode's key features. Electron allows for a modular approach, where new features can be added easily without affecting the core app.

3. Slack (Electron and Node.js)

Slack is a messaging platform for teams, and it uses both **Electron** for its desktop app and **Node.js** for its backend services. Slack's decision to use Electron for the desktop version allowed it to deliver a consistent experience across multiple platforms, including Windows, macOS, and Linux.

How Slack Uses Electron and Node.js:

- **Electron for Desktop**: Slack uses Electron to create cross-platform desktop apps with the same codebase, offering native-like performance and integrating well with the underlying operating system.

- **Node.js Backend**: The backend of Slack is powered by **Node.js**, which is used to handle real-time communication, message storage, and scaling the app to handle millions of active users.

Lessons from Slack's Use of Electron and Node.js:

- **Real-Time Communication**: Node.js's ability to handle **asynchronous I/O** operations is critical for real-time apps like Slack. It allows the app to handle large numbers of concurrent connections with low latency.

- **Cross-Platform Desktop Experience**: Electron allows Slack to create a consistent, native-like experience across platforms while simplifying the development process by sharing the same codebase.

Project: Building a Real-World Project from Scratch

Now that we've seen how successful apps use **React Native**, **Electron**, and **Node.js**, let's go through the process of building a **real-world app** from scratch. We will build a **project**

management app that allows users to create and manage tasks, collaborate with others, and track progress.

In this project, we will integrate all the technologies we've covered so far:

- **React Native** for the mobile app.

- **Electron** for the desktop app.

- **Node.js** for the backend.

Step 1: Setting Up the Backend (Node.js)

1. **Initialize a Node.js Project:** First, create a new Node.js project in your desired directory:

bash

```
mkdir project-manager
cd project-manager
npm init -y
```

2. **Install Dependencies**: Install the necessary dependencies for your backend, including **Express** for creating the API and **MongoDB** for storing project data.

bash

```
npm install express mongoose body-parser cors
```

3. **Create the API**: In your server.js file, create routes for creating projects, adding tasks, and updating task statuses:

javascript

```
const express =
require('express');
const mongoose =
require('mongoose');
const bodyParser = require('body-parser');
const cors = require('cors');
```

```
const app = express();
app.use(bodyParser.json());
app.use(cors());

mongoose.connect('mongodb://localh
ost:27017/projectManager', {
useNewUrlParser: true,
useUnifiedTopology: true });

const taskSchema = new
mongoose.Schema({
  name: String,
  status: String,
});

const projectSchema = new
mongoose.Schema({
  name: String,
  description: String,
  tasks: [taskSchema],
```

```
});

const Project =
mongoose.model('Project',
projectSchema);

app.post('/projects', async (req,
res) => {
  const { name, description } =
req.body;
  const project = new Project({
name, description, tasks: [] });
  await project.save();
  res.status(201).send(project);
});

app.post('/projects/:id/tasks',
async (req, res) => {
  const project = await
Project.findById(req.params.id);
  const { name } = req.body;
```

```
  const task = { name, status:
'Pending' };
  project.tasks.push(task);
  await project.save();
  res.status(201).send(task);
});


app.listen(5000, () => {
  console.log('Server is running
on port 5000');
});
```

This backend allows users to create projects and add tasks to them. It uses **MongoDB** to store the project data and **Express** to serve the API.

Step 2: Building the Mobile App (React Native)

1. **Create a New React Native Project:**

```bash
bash
```

```
npx react-native init
ProjectManagerMobile
cd ProjectManagerMobile
```

2. **Install Axios**: You'll need **Axios** to make API requests to the Node.js backend:

```bash
bash
```

```
npm install axios
```

3. **Create the UI for the Mobile App**: In App.js, create the UI to display projects and tasks, and allow the user to add new projects and tasks.

```javascript
javascript
```

```javascript
import React, { useState,
useEffect } from 'react';
import { View, Text, Button,
TextInput, FlatList, StyleSheet }
from 'react-native';
import axios from 'axios';
```

```
const App = () => {
  const [projects, setProjects] =
useState([]);
  const [newProjectName,
setNewProjectName] = useState('');
  const [newTaskName,
setNewTaskName] = useState('');
  const [selectedProjectId,
setSelectedProjectId] =
useState(null);

  useEffect(() => {

axios.get('http://localhost:5000/p
rojects')
      .then((response) =>
setProjects(response.data));
  }, []);

  const addProject = () => {
```

```
axios.post('http://localhost:5000/
projects', { name: newProjectName,
description: '' })
      .then((response) => {
        setProjects([...projects,
response.data]);
        setNewProjectName('');
      });
  };


  const addTask = () => {

axios.post(`http://localhost:5000/
projects/${selectedProjectId}/task
s`, { name: newTaskName })
      .then((response) => {
        const updatedProjects =
projects.map((project) =>
          project._id ===
selectedProjectId
```

```
            ? { ...project, tasks:
[...project.tasks, response.data]
}
            : project
    );


setProjects(updatedProjects);
      setNewTaskName('');
    });
  };


  return (
    <View
style={styles.container}>
      <Text>Project Manager</Text>

      <TextInput
        style={styles.input}
        placeholder="New Project
Name"
        value={newProjectName}
```

```
onChangeText={setNewProjectName}
    />
    <Button title="Add Project"
onPress={addProject} />

    <FlatList
      data={projects}
      renderItem={({ item }) =>
(
        <View>

<Text>{item.name}</Text>
          <Button title="Select
Project" onPress={() =>
setSelectedProjectId(item._id)} />
          <FlatList
            data={item.tasks}
            renderItem={({ item
}) => <Text>{item.name}</Text>}
```

```
            keyExtractor={(task)
=> task.name}
        />
        </View>
      )}
      keyExtractor={(item) =>
item._id}
      />


      {selectedProjectId && (
        <View>
          <TextInput
            style={styles.input}
            placeholder="New Task
Name"
            value={newTaskName}

onChangeText={setNewTaskName}
          />
          <Button title="Add Task"
onPress={addTask} />
```

```
        </View>
      )}
    </View>
  );
};


const styles = StyleSheet.create({
  container: {
    flex: 1,
    padding: 20,
  },
  input: {
    height: 40,
    borderColor: 'gray',
    borderWidth: 1,
    marginBottom: 10,
    paddingLeft: 10,
  },
});


export default App;
```

This code will display a list of projects, allow the user to add new projects, and then add tasks to the selected project.

Step 3: Building the Desktop App (Electron)

1. **Create a New Electron Project**: Follow similar steps as before to create your **Electron** app. This app will have similar functionality as the mobile app but with a desktop UI using **HTML** and **JavaScript**.

2. **Setup API Calls**: Use **Axios** to make API requests to the Node.js backend from your Electron app, similar to what we did with the mobile app.

Lessons from the Field: Common Challenges and Solutions

As you develop cross-platform applications, you will inevitably encounter challenges. Some of the most common challenges developers face when building cross-platform apps include:

1. Performance Issues

Solution: Use tools like **React Native Performance Monitor** and **Electron's Developer Tools** to profile and optimize performance. Implement **lazy loading**, optimize memory usage, and use asynchronous operations to keep the app responsive.

2. Platform-Specific Bugs

Solution: When building cross-platform apps, always test on both platforms to catch platform-specific issues early. Use platform-specific code where necessary (e.g., using Platform.OS in React Native).

3. Synchronizing Data Across Platforms

Solution: Use tools like **Redux** and **Apollo Client** for state management to ensure data is synchronized across platforms. Use **local storage** to cache data when offline, and ensure data syncs when the internet is available.

Conclusion

In this chapter, we've looked at successful real-world cross-platform apps, explored how they were built, and walked through a **project-based learning exercise** to build a real-world app. We've also discussed common challenges in cross-platform development and shared practical solutions.

By analyzing case studies, building real-world applications, and learning from developers' experiences, you now have the skills and insights to tackle complex, cross-platform projects with confidence. Keep experimenting, stay curious, and soon you'll be building your own successful apps!

Chapter 12: Next Steps and Continuing Your Journey

Software development is an exciting and ever-evolving field. As technology continues to grow, so does the potential for innovation and improvement. Whether you are just starting your journey into cross-platform development or looking to further expand your skill set, the key to long-term success lies in continuous learning and growth. This chapter will guide you on how to stay updated in the rapidly changing tech landscape, explore advanced topics and future technologies, and inspire you as you take your next steps in the world of software development.

Staying Updated in the Ever-Changing Tech Landscape

The world of software development is constantly evolving. New frameworks, libraries, tools, and best practices are introduced every year, making it challenging to keep up. However, staying updated is essential for continued success in the field. Here are some strategies to help you stay on top of trends and continue learning as a developer.

1. Follow Industry Blogs and Websites

The best way to stay informed about the latest trends in cross-platform development is to follow industry blogs and websites. These resources often publish articles, tutorials, and case studies that can help you learn about new technologies, tools, and best practices.

Some popular websites and blogs to follow include:

- **Dev.to**: A community of developers sharing articles, tutorials, and project ideas.

- **Medium**: A popular platform where many developers publish their insights, tutorials, and reflections on industry trends.

- **React Native Blog**: The official blog for React Native, offering updates, feature releases, and best practices.

- **CSS-Tricks**: A great resource for web development, including front-end technologies that can influence cross-platform development.

2. Engage in Online Communities

Online communities provide a wealth of knowledge, and engaging with them can help you learn from others, ask questions, and stay current. Communities like **Stack Overflow**, **GitHub**, and **Reddit** are excellent for connecting with other developers, discussing new tools, and finding solutions to coding challenges.

Here are a few online communities to explore:

- **Stack Overflow**: A question-and-answer site where you can find solutions to specific coding issues or contribute your knowledge.

- **GitHub**: Explore open-source repositories to see how other developers are solving problems, and contribute to projects to improve your skills.

- **Reddit**: Subreddits like r/reactnative, r/javascript, and r/webdev are great places to find tutorials, discuss new technologies, and share your projects.

- **Discord and Slack Channels**: Many communities have dedicated channels for developers, providing a more real-time platform for conversation and help.

3. Take Online Courses and Tutorials

While reading articles and engaging in communities is a great way to stay informed, sometimes a structured approach can provide a more in-depth understanding of a topic. Platforms like **Udemy**, **Coursera**, **freeCodeCamp**, and **Pluralsight** offer courses on the latest technologies and tools used in cross-platform development.

Here are a few courses to consider:

- **React Native Development with Hooks and Context:** Learn the latest React Native features like hooks, context, and state management.

- **The Complete Guide to Building Serverless Applications:** A course that teaches how to build scalable applications using serverless architecture.

- **Modern Web Development with GraphQL:** A deep dive into using GraphQL, one of the most innovative technologies for managing APIs.

By committing to lifelong learning, you ensure that your skills remain relevant and that you can leverage the latest technologies to build better applications.

4. Attend Conferences and Meetups

Attending conferences and meetups is a fantastic way to learn from industry leaders, engage with other developers, and discover the latest tools and technologies. Conferences can offer insight into upcoming trends, new tools, and key topics for cross-platform development.

- **React Native EU**: An annual conference focused on React Native development, featuring talks, workshops, and networking opportunities.

- **JSConf**: A conference for JavaScript developers, including topics related to frameworks like React Native, Node.js, and more.

- **Google I/O and Apple WWDC**: Both of these major conferences highlight new trends, tools, and frameworks in mobile and cross-platform development.

If you can't attend in person, many conferences are streamed online, offering virtual tickets that allow you to watch the talks and sessions from home.

5. Experiment with New Tools and Libraries

One of the most effective ways to stay up-to-date is by actively experimenting with new tools, libraries, and frameworks. As new features are released in React Native, Node.js, Electron, and other technologies, take the time to integrate them into your projects and explore their capabilities.

For instance, consider trying:

- **React Native Paper**: A library for building material design components in React Native.

- **Expo**: A framework and platform for universal React apps that simplify the development and deployment process.

- **Next.js**: A framework for React that simplifies server-side rendering and routing.

- **Electron Forge**: A toolkit for building and packaging Electron apps with ease.

By experimenting with new tools, you stay ahead of the curve and become more adaptable as the development landscape evolves.

Advanced Topics and Future Technologies

While React Native, Node.js, and Electron are powerful tools for building cross-platform apps, there are many advanced concepts and emerging technologies that you should explore to future-proof your development skills. In this section, we'll dive into some of these advanced topics and explain how they can enhance your cross-platform development projects.

1. Progressive Web Apps (PWAs)

Progressive Web Apps (PWAs) combine the best features of mobile apps and websites. PWAs are websites that behave like native mobile apps, offering offline functionality, push notifications, and fast load times, all without needing to be installed through an app store.

Key Features of PWAs:

- **Offline Support**: PWAs can work offline by caching assets and data, ensuring that users can access the app even when they don't have an internet connection.

- **Push Notifications**: PWAs can send notifications to users, similar to native apps, allowing for real-time engagement.

- **App-like Experience**: PWAs provide a seamless, app-like experience in a web browser, including smooth animations and responsive layouts.

How to Build a PWA:

To build a PWA with React, you can use **Create React App** with PWA support, or use **Next.js** for server-side rendering and better performance.

Example of registering a service worker in a React app:

```
javascript
```

```
if ('serviceWorker' in navigator)
{
  window.addEventListener('load',
() => {

navigator.serviceWorker.register('
/service-
worker.js').then((registration) =>
{
    console.log('Service Worker
registered:', registration);
   }).catch((error) => {
    console.log('Service Worker
registration failed:', error);
   });
  });
}
```

PWAs are a powerful tool for creating cross-platform applications without the need to publish them on app stores. They work on both desktop and mobile browsers, making them a great choice for many modern web apps.

2. GraphQL

GraphQL is a query language for APIs that enables clients to request exactly the data they need, which can significantly improve the efficiency of data fetching compared to traditional REST APIs. It is especially useful for cross-platform development where multiple clients (mobile, web, desktop) need to access the same backend.

Benefits of GraphQL:

- **Flexible Queries**: Clients can specify exactly which fields they need, reducing over-fetching and under-fetching of data.

- **Single Request**: With GraphQL, you can retrieve all the data your app needs in a single request, unlike **REST**, where multiple endpoints are often required.

- **Real-Time Updates**: Using **GraphQL subscriptions**, you can receive real-time updates as data changes on the server.

How to Implement GraphQL:

Here's a simple setup for GraphQL in a Node.js app using **Apollo Server:**

```bash
bash
```

```
npm install apollo-server graphql
javascript
```

```javascript
const { ApolloServer, gql } =
require('apollo-server');

const typeDefs = gql`
  type Query {
    hello: String
```

```
  }
`;


const resolvers = {
  Query: {
    hello: () => 'Hello world!',
  },
};


const server = new ApolloServer({
typeDefs, resolvers });


server.listen().then(({ url }) =>
{
  console.log(`Server running at
${url}`);
});
```

You can now query the server with the following GraphQL query:

```
graphql
```

```
{
  hello
}
```

GraphQL is ideal for cross-platform apps because it allows clients to request only the data they need, resulting in faster load times and a more efficient API.

3. Serverless Architecture

Serverless architecture allows you to build and run applications without managing servers. With serverless, the cloud provider manages the infrastructure for you, allowing you to focus on writing code and deploying it in a scalable, cost-efficient manner.

Benefits of Serverless:

- **No Server Management**: You don't need to worry about provisioning, scaling, or managing servers.

- **Scalable**: Serverless functions automatically scale based on demand, ensuring that your app can handle traffic spikes without manual intervention.

- **Cost-Efficient**: You only pay for the compute power you use, rather than maintaining servers 24/7.

How to Build Serverless Apps:

Platforms like **AWS Lambda, Google Cloud Functions**, and **Azure Functions** enable you to build serverless applications. Here's an example of deploying a simple function using AWS Lambda:

1. **Create the Lambda Function**: Use the AWS Lambda console or CLI to create a new function.

2. **Write the Code**: Write your function code in Node.js or another supported runtime.

3. **Deploy the Function:** Deploy the function to AWS Lambda and connect it to other services (like **API Gateway** or **S3**) to trigger the function.

Serverless architecture is ideal for handling API requests, processing background jobs, and performing complex computations without worrying about server management.

Final Thoughts and Inspiration for the Future

As you conclude this journey through cross-platform app development, it's important to reflect on the skills you've learned and the many exciting opportunities ahead. Building cross-platform apps with **React Native, Electron,** and **Node.js** is just the beginning. The tools and technologies we've explored in this book lay the foundation for creating powerful, scalable, and maintainable apps across all platforms.

Inspiration for Future Projects

The world of software development is filled with endless possibilities. With the knowledge and confidence you've gained, you are now equipped to take on a wide range of projects, from building your own personal apps to launching a startup. Whether you want to create a mobile app for your business, build a desktop app for a niche market, or contribute to open-source projects, the skills you've acquired will serve you well.

Continuing Your Learning Journey

Remember, technology never stops evolving. Always stay curious and continue to experiment with new tools and technologies. Follow industry blogs, contribute to open-source projects, and challenge yourself to build bigger and better apps.

You now have the tools to bring your ideas to life—so go ahead and make it happen! The possibilities are endless.

Conclusion

In this final chapter, we've explored how to stay updated in the tech world, dove into advanced topics like PWAs, GraphQL, and serverless architecture, and provided inspiration for the future. As you continue your journey, remember to keep learning, stay engaged with the developer community, and never stop building. Whether you're building a career or working on a personal project, the knowledge you've gained here will be a stepping stone toward future success. Best of luck in your next steps, and keep creating amazing cross-platform applications!

www.ingramcontent.com/pod-product-compliance
Lightning Source LLC
La Vergne TN
LVHW051437050326
832903LV00030BD/3126